Tamm's Textbook Tools

Student workbook containing worksheets and course materials for use with:

AP* Psychology

Myers' Psychology for AP$^+$ 2nd edition (green cover)

Coursepak Series A   **Independently Made**

David Tamm

Copyrights

When given as a full workbook, this material improves content coherency, student enjoyment, parent appreciation, and teacher satisfaction."

-State of Florida Certified Teacher

Contents

This resource book is organized in the following way to integrate with Myers' Psychology for AP 2nd edition:

"A giant leap for studentkind"

"Awesome, usable resources!"

"Spend 1 hour's pay, save 300 hours' planning time!"

"Engaging. Students pointedly interact with the book's features."

Suggested Use

Manic Moonday

It is recommended that students have a lecture overview of the key points in each module to be done that week, which is going to be 1-6, depending on size and import. The lecture may take the form of a conversation, linking the concepts to regular life situations. While teachers are discouraged in many parts of the country from lecturing, the speed of the AP Psychology course necessitates some direct transmission of content. Perhaps minor grades could be assigned for notes? Part I vocab sheets can always be used as a guide during discussion.

Textbook Tiw's Day

Most school districts encourage pair or group work. This can be used to positive effect if students mine the textbook or a review book in class. They can either jigsaw the chapter, presenting their take on part of the whole, or jointly venture to find the answers to the specific questions, such as those provided here for each module.

Writing Woden's Day

The AP Psych curriculum is writing intensive, of course, and a good way to build up key thinking processes related to navigating one's way through writing topics, is to brainstorm and diagram solutions to the FRQs located at the end of the modules in the Myers book. Another helpful way to practice looking for evidence and building a case is good old-fashioned reading comprehension. As many teachers know, however, the content of the passages is key. If you find this work helpful and of high quality, check out the companion volume to this book, *Tamm's Textbook Tools Coursepak C: The Grand Tour of Psychology,* on *Amazon.com* or another platform. Bolt's resource binder is helpful in locating interesting demonstrations and other activities. If you don't have it, try and find it. If you are homeschooling, contact *Tamm's Textbook Tools* on Facebook or email, and we'll see what we can do.

Technetronic Thor's Day

Many AP teachers try to bring in technology to the classroom, whether in the form of a laptop cart, or by taking students to a media lab. Increasingly, students are just using their mobile devices. *Kahoot.it* is now popular as a Jeopardy-style review game, joining *Quizlet* and a vast number of other review materials available online. A good directory to websites usable with AP Psychology classes, including the psychedelic 'groovy' site and Myers' textbook site with Psychsim activities, is located at Antarcticaedu.com/psy.htm. Included in the addendum to this volume is a Crash Course viewer response sheet that can be given as homework on Thursday nights, or completed as an in-class review assignment.

Fantastic Frige's Day

It is suggested that students take a 50-question test once a week. That means combining modules during the week. A 35 min. period should be reserved in class- or in some cases out- to do these weekly tests. If this happens on Friday, it is recommended students take home the vocab sheet for the next module home for homework, due the following Monday. A test corrections sheet for some amount of extra points is included in this bundle.

*These assignments can certainly be given as a homework battery all year

Suggested Year Plan

Week 1: modules 1
Week 2: modules 2, 3
Week 3: modules 4, 5
Week 4: modules 6, 7, 8
Week 5: modules 9, 10
Week 6: modules 11, 12, 13
Week 7: modules 14, 15
Week 8: modules 16, 17
Week 9: modules 18, 19, 20, 21
Week 10: modules 22, 23, 24
Week 11: modules 25, 81
Week 12: modules 26
Week 13: modules 27, 28, 29, 30
Week 14: modules 31, 32, 33
Week 15: modules 34, 35, 36
Week 16: modules 37, 38, 39, 40
Week 17: modules 41, 42, 43, 44
Week 18: modules 45, 46, 47, 48, 49, 50
Week 19: modules 51, 52, 53, 54
Week 20: modules 55, 56
Week 21: modules 57, 58, 59
Week 22: modules 60, 61
Week 23: modules 62, 63, 64
Week 24: modules 65, 66
Week 25: modules 67, 68, 69
Week 26: modules 70, 71, 72
Week 27: modules 73
Week 28: modules 74, 75
Week 29: modules 76, 77
Week 30: modules 78, 79, 80
Week 31: modules 82, 83, 84, 85

Extra Weekly Projects

WEEK 1, MODULE 1: Have students break into groups and have each group make a poster looking at a psychological topic from a certain perspective (i.e.: psychoanalytical, behaviorist)... Locate and watch the first 45 min. of Charles Osgood's *In Search of Ourselves.* You might also do the Introspection activity, where a piece of candy is distributed and students write their sensory reactions to the candy in as much excruciating detail as possible. You also may do the 'Dinner with a Dead Psychologist' activity, in which students pair up and report what questions they determined to ask the psychologist, and how they think he or she would answer them. View Crash Course Psychology episode #1.

WEEK 2, MODULES 2, 3: Do the Outrageous Celebrity project, whereby students examine the behaviors/motivations of a notorious figure in the public spotlight, and try to explain their attitudes and actions from a specific psychological approach, or a combination of many. Examples abound, Lady Gaga is a popular one, Dennis Rodman (though a bit dated), etc. Have them collect images of their transformation to outrageousness. Ask them to rationalize the behavior/attitude as well. How might Freud explain it vs. Skinner, Rogers, Beck or Bandura? Have them construct a three-pronged biopsychosocial chart for it at the end. Do the Psychsim Lab: Psychology's Timeline (see addendum for website addresses).

WEEK 3, MODULES 4, 5: Have students brainstorm what research method (survey, case study, naturalistic observation, etc.) would be most appropriate for actual inquiries into some psychological or social phenomena. Examine pitfalls in survey questions, like bias, complex wording, etc. Students might also do naturalistic observation in the cafeteria at lunch. If you have Bolt's resource binder (or if you don't, have students make a list of all the presidents of the USA and their age at inauguration)- and then have them make a bar graph of all the presidents inaugurated in their 40's, 50's, 60's and 70's. Then have students calculate the mean age, median age and the mode. Get a clip of James Randi challenging Yri Geller on his spoon bending on the Tonight Show with Johnny Carson to illustrate the scientific attitude. Carl Sagan was a big proponent of this as well, and you can see it on Youtube's *The Sagan Series.* Do Psychsim Lab: Descriptive Statistics.

WEEK 4, MODULES 6, 7, 8: If you have the Bolt binder (and if not your school should buy it for you), do the Nuts and Bolts demonstration to illustrate data collection, the Yardstick experiment to demonstrate experimenter bias (when you cheat and let the boy win, then claim boys have better reflexes), and the correlation project with hair length in inches vs. number of shoes owned, to demonstrate how to place data on a scatterplot (and the concept of confounding variables due to the fact that the long hair did not *cause* the number of shoes to go up). Something else did. You could do hair loss vs. years of marriage too, 'find a correlation,' and use the data to bolster your false hypothesis that too much commitment makes a guy's hair fall out! Studies show... Finally, looking at ethics issues in experiments of the past is a good platform for debate on what should be allowed to happen for the good of psychological science. Search for notorious experiments in the history of psychology as a guide. If you want some entertainment you can look into serious ethics violations like stolen cadavers (Hare, Burke, Knox case), and have students identify why this experiment wouldn't pass committee peer review today. Crash Course Psychology episode #2. Psychsim Lab: Correlation and Psychsim Lab: What's Wrong with this Picture.

WEEK 5, MODULES 9, 10: Take time to diagram a neuron on the board, draw it out with the students and label each part, describe its function, and run a simulation from dendrite to the release of neurotransmitters into the next synaptic gap. You could do the 'Neuron Dance' where students line the back of the room holding one-another's forearms and cannot 'activate' until the previous neuron had 'fired.' One at a time, the students 'fire' and move their arms in a wave pattern. You may have them not touch each other to simulate the synaptic gap. The film *Awakenings* with Robin Williams and Robert de Niro goes with this section. You might also show the clip of Lou Gehrig giving his famous "Luckiest Man" speech after being diagnosed with the mysterious disease called MS. Search for articles on oxytocin by Nicholas Wade and Kevin MacDonald for the 'revenge of biology' perspective. Crash Course Psychology episode #3. Psychsim Lab: Neural Messages.

WEEK 6, MODULES 11, 12, 13: Take time to diagram the whole brain on the board, starting with 'lower brain', then limbic system, then cerebellum, then the cerebral cortex. Emphasize the corpus callosum as an 'east-west' nerve highway from right to left hemispheres, and the thalamus as a 'north-south' nerve highway from lower to upper brain. Students may jigsaw a brain part, one for each or one per peer-group, and then discuss its function and significance in psychology. The Wagner Preference Inventory can be done to see which hemisphere, if any, the survey taker favors. Watch Yale lecture #2. Crash Course Psychology episode #4. Psychsim Lab: Brain and Behavior, Hemispheric Specialization and Dueling Brains.

WEEK 7, MODULES 14, 15: Talking about psychology from the evolutionary perspective can take many forms. If you are daring, you can mention E.O. Wilson's *Sociobiology* and how much controversy it caused in the 1970s and 80s at the apex of environmentalism. You can mention Charles Murray and Richard Herrnstein's *The Bell Curve* and the controversy it caused in the 1990s, the controversy surrounding psychologists Richard Lynn, J. Philippe Rushton and Kevin MacDonald in the 2000s, and Satoshi Kanazawa, Nicholas Wade, Frank Salter, and DNA discoverer James Watson in the 2010s. Have students pick a trait people have, from tendency to cooperate to aggression to care for young to various phobias, and determine likely reasons that particular trait exists as it does in people today. What was/is its survival value? Also, with Nature-Nurture, have students evaluate how much of height (90%), intelligence (75%) and personality/character (50%) is inherited vs. from environment. You may also discuss a recent article on selecting the traits of babies, increasingly offered by labs at home and abroad. Genetic modification is an underlying theme in the movie *Starship Troopers,* which portrays a society in which eugenic selection of human beings has been implemented. High school students run genetic scans on each other as if it were a game, and the results compare boys and girls, and give them a 'genetic compatibility score,' which students will find interesting. Watch Yale lecture 10. Psychsim Lab: Mind Reading Monkeys. No Crash Course for this week.

WEEK 8, MODULES 16, 17: Students can brainstorm times they did bottom-up vs. top-down processing. You can diagram the eye in detail on the board, imagining a light wave's journey to transduction and the journey of the impulse to the feature detectors and visual cortex- and students could copy it on a blank piece of paper, perhaps color-coding it. The book *Teaching Tips for General Psychology* has a few good ideas for sensation. Crash Course Psychology episodes #5 and 6. Psychsim Lab: Colorful World.

WEEK 9, MODULES 18, 19, 20, 21: Using brain teasers and visual illusions readily findable online, have students determine which parts of the sense and perception process the illusions are 'fooling', or it may be a concept they are illustrating. People will not all formulate the same perception, so you can talk about 'truth' as an absolute value vs. being relative to what someone perceives, i.e.: 'in the eye of the beholder.' Is there anything we know is true cognitively that we do not perceive as such? You could also find a magic trickster or card dealer who tricks perceptions, or use the video of the woman sauntering across a basketball game with an umbrella (or in another variation in a gorilla suit). If you like, have students sketch out the ear, and compare what happens to a sound wave with what happens to a light wave. When does transduction occur? Etc. Yale lecture 7, 11 and guest lecture 1 are appropriate this week. Crash Course Psychology episode #7. Psychsim Lab: Visual Illusions and Auditory System.

WEEK 10, MODULES 22, 23, 24: Taking a graphic journey of a night's sleep on the board, hour by hour and cycle by cycle, is an informative way to teach the waves, states and circadian rhythm. Have students recall their dreams and write them, then look for common themes and things that happen in dreams, and discuss whether Freud was right about manifest and latent content. Give the Morningness-Eveningness Questionarire to see if the person is a night owl or a morning lark. Movies about sleep and dreams include *Inception* and *Total Recall.* Yale lecture 17 works here. Crash Course Psychology episodes #8 and 9. Psychsim Lab: EEG and Sleep Stages.

WEEK 11, MODULES 25, 81: With drugs you can assign groups to investigate different ones, and report to the class. The class can classify it, see the negative side yet also the motivation people have to abuse it. Be sure to make clear the different forms of addition, and connect it to all the biopsychosocial reasons people use, legally and illegally. 'Spiders on Drugs' is a humorous Youtube video if there are 5 extra minutes. If you can, get a cop to come in and give a presentation on what drugs do to the community you live in. If you want to make an even stronger point about this section, you could do the Icekube Addiction activity by Charles Blair-Broeker, whereby students have to keep ice in its solid form around them throughout the day, and you are their "dealer" with a large supply in your room. They fiend for it and have to get out of class or lunch or anything, just to get their fix from you- and hide their problem from others- an apt simulation of addiction. Movies? We should mention movies about alcohol and drug addiction. There are a lot of them but a few stand out. *The Lost Weekend* about alcohol addition (1945) is one. The movie won the Oscar for best director and best actor. Find it on Youtube or Amazon. In *28 Days*, Sandra Bullock plays an alcohol addict in rehab, demonstrating the therapy process. *Trainspotting, Blow, Easy Rider, The Doors* and *Requiem for a Dream* are movies about drug addiction. The Star Trek: The Next Generation episode *The Game* looks at addiction to a game, an 80s premonition of our own addictions to virtual realities, one of which being video games. Crash Course Psychology episode #10. Psychsim Lab: Your Mind on Drugs.

WEEK 12, MODULE 26: Youtube videos of the Pavlov and Watson experiments are good follow-ups to the classical conditioning discussion. A clip from *The Office* TV show (search Jim conditions Dwight) is a humorous short. Have students think about other times they and people in general are classically conditioned. Take the Sensitivity to Punishment and Reward Questionnaire. Yale lecture 3 is appropriate this week. Crash Course Psychology episode #11. Psychsim Lab: Classical Conditioning and Maze Learning.

WEEK 13, MODULES 27, 28, 29, 30: Youtube videos of the Thorndike Puzzle Box and Skinner Pigeon experiments are helpful, along with a humorous clip from Big Bang Theory (Search: Big Bang Theory Conditioning) where the friend does operant conditioning on the girlfriend of his roommate. Have students figure out what reinforcement schedules are used in a variety of cases (i.e.: gambling is variable ratio, conditioning Penny with chocolate candies is fixed ratio). If it happens to be Thanksgiving or Christmas break, or if you are willing to spend two class periods on a full-length movie, *Bedtime for Bonzo* (1951) examines the Nature-nurture issue at the height of behaviorism. Ronald Reagan stars as Professor Boyd, who wants to marry the daughter of the dean, and the dean finds out Boyd's dad was in jail- an indication Boyd had criminal genes he doesn't want in his family. The bad old nature guy finally comes around to the power of environment at the end, but with a few twists that students love.

This movie is cheap on *Amazon*. An article on observational learning and the latest on how TV/movie/video game violence affects kids would work here. Find Amy Sutherland's NY Times article *What Shamu Taught me about a Happy Marriage* and have students marvel at a lady who did operant condition on her husband as if he were a circus animal… and it worked. Yale lecture 4 is appropriate this week. Crash Course Psychology episode #12. Psychsim Lab: Operant Conditioning, Monkey See, Monkey Do, and Helplessly Hoping.

WEEK 14, MODULES 31, 32, 33: Have students graph 1-6 on the x-axis and 0-18 on the y-axis. Do the demo where they pair up and one has six trials of 10 seconds each to memorize a random 18-digit number you put on the board in big font. Cover it with the screen or something else after each 10-second viewing. The learners then speak the number back to the recorder, and the recorder marks how many were spoken back correctly, between 0 and 18. This well-used demo is very good because it can illustrate many of the concepts in 7a, like serial position effect, etc. Also, do the Seven Dwarves recall game. Give them 30 seconds to write all the names they remember, and in round two speak out the names of 20, including 13 false names you make up like 'Slappy' or 'Tired.' Then have them get the concepts of recall vs. recognition, and why fill in the blank tests are harder than multiple choice. You can also do the demo on words related to sleeping and nighttime, available in Bolt's binder. For flashbulb memories, try having them think of their own, and also things for different generations in history, i.e.: Pearl Harbor, JFK blown away, Apollo Moon landing, 9/11, etc. If you'd like to see a movie for this section, try *Memento, Fifty First Dates, Limitless, Finding Nemo, Robocop, the Bourne Identity, The Butterfly Effect,* or *The Notebook* (Alzheimer's disease). Yale lecture 8 is appropriate this week. Crash Course Psychology episodes #13 and 14. Psychsim Lab: Iconic Memory, Short Term Memory, Forgetting, Trusting Your Memory and When Memory Fails.

WEEK 15, MODULES 34, 35, 36: Bolt's binder has a good one on problem solving that is also online if you don't have the binder. Students like the Buddhist Monk Problem, the Truthtellers and Liars Problem, and the Hobbits and Orcs problem. For language, there is an opportunity to read a review of Pinker's *The Language Instinct* and then Theodore Dalrymple's *The Gift of Language,* which argues against some of Pinker's claims about facility for language being mostly inborn. Star Trek: The Next Generation tackled miscommunication in *Darmok,* an episode when the crew meets an alien race that speaks in metaphors, not in semantic structures familiar to humans. An assignment to this episode is included in the addendum. You can find clips on Youtube or watch the whole thing. The movie *Good Will Hunting* involves a gifted person being discovered by psychology professionals and channeled into realizing his potential. Yale lecture 6 is appropriate this week. Crash Course Psychology episodes #15 and 16. Psychsim Lab: My Head is Spinning.

WEEK 16, MODULES 37, 38, 39, 40: If you or your class are shy, this is not your chapter. It has Freud's psychosexual stages, discussions of the incidence of homosexuality, the sex motivation of males for spreading their DNA around to as many different nubile females as possible, and the motivation for females to secure comfort and prosperity by ensnaring an alpha male. How to approach it? Focus on hunger and the hypothalamus messing with the body's equilibrium! You can also look at how advertising motivates us to buy stuff we probably don't need. There is a good sheet on this in the *Teaching Tips for General Psychology* book. Give students the Exploration Inventory, and have them assess where they are on Maslow's hierarchy, relating it to motivations in their present day. If you are interested in gender, sexual orientation and identity, *The Birdcage* takes a humorous look at how heterosexual and homosexual people see each other, while *What Women Want* looks at how men and women see each other differently. A movie for eating disorders is *Girl, Interrupted.* Yale lecture 14 and guest lecture 2 are appropriate this week. Another movie worth seeing for the post-Freud Psychodynamic school is *Finding Joe,* about heroism and overcoming personal troubles through tapping into the Jungian archetype present but partially hidden within oneself. This is presented through an analysis of the teachings of Joseph Campbell, the foremost mythologist of the 20th century. You can also Youtube his videos series called *The Power of Myth,* which covers many topics. Crash Course Psychology episodes #17, 27 and 33. Psychsim Lab: Hunger and the Fat Rat, and Catching Liars.

WEEK 17, MODULES 41, 42, 43, 44: Debating the three theories is a good start, but find online the reasons each group of theorists obtained their opinion on the matter. Ekman's universal expressions data is watchable on Youtube, and a good talk can be based on what each emotion conveys worldwide, and which ones differ by culture or country. Happiness and how to obtain it, Myers' specialty, can be found in documentaries on Youtube and Netflix. The *Star Trek* episode *The Enemy Within* can be found to show the captain becoming two people, one full of raw emotion and the other without enough of it, a yin-yang situation. Consequences ensue and the moral is that a healthy balance is best. A clip about Phineas Gage is appropriate here. Give the Need for Affect Scale to check their level of proneness to emotionality. On Youtube, get a 1950s perspective on emotions by searching: *Psychology Coronet.* This company made school documentaries that are informative for us today because they give a window into how things were different. Students like the one called "Controlling Your Emotions," as well as "Understanding Emotions" and "Overcoming Fear." Finally, National Geographic's *Portrait of a Killer,* is a good look at Robert Sapolsky's work fin iguring out how stress hurts us over time. Do the *Psychinquiry* lesson on Stress Level at: http://ebooks.bfwpub.com/psychinquiry. Yale lecture 9 and 10 are appropriate this week. Crash Course Psychology episodes #25 and 26. Psychsim Lab: Expressing Emotion and All Stressed Out.

WEEK 18, MODULES 45, 46, 47, 48: Discuss the stages of prenatal development- there are plenty of clips for this- and the Piaget stages. If your school can afford it, obtain *Inside Out Psychology,* a video series featuring David Myers and a whole host of top psychologists. Warning: it is expensive. Have students note the key changes and abilities in each Piaget stage, and debate whether stage theories are valid models of human development on the escalator vs. stairs comparison. You can have students recall scenes and events that made impressions on them in each year of their childhood, from 3 on. Have them reflect on what they thought about, their moral standing if they had one, and what they were interested in (motivation) in each grade. Call it "The Years of Life" or something like that. Give them the Parental Authority Questionnaire Pertaining to Mothers to see if they can identify their mom's parenting style. *Breakfast Club* is a movie showing the teenage identity crisis. Yale lecture 5 is good here. Crash Course Psychology episodes #18 and 19. Psychsim Lab: Conception to Birth and Cognitive Development.

WEEK 19, MODULES 51, 52, 53, 54: *The Real Roots of the Midlife Crisis* by Rouch in *The Atlantic* examines that secular malady in which people wake up one day and ask "is this all there is?" If you are brave, you can show clips from *American Beauty* when Kevin Spacey manifests symptoms of a midlife crisis. Have students ponder what might give them a midlife crisis if they do not accomplish it. Have them fill out the Life/Values/Goals survey, imagining they are on the verge of finishing their time as fellow travelers on the Spaceship Earth, which gets them thinking. *What Dreams May Come* is about coming to terms with death, while Yale does a class on dying, findable online at: http://antarcticaedu.com/opencourseengineering.htm. Yale lecture 12, 15 fits here. On Youtube, search *Coronet "Self-Conscious Guy"* and see the identity issue, followed by *"Psychological Maturity: Act Your Age,"* and *"How Friendly are You?"* for a 1950s perspective. Older adulthood is portrayed in the film *Grumpy Old Men.* Crash Course Psychology episode #20. Psychsim Lab: Who am I? and Signs of Ageing.

WEEK 20, MODULES 55, 56: Students can analyze examples of all the Freudian defense mechanisms and explain what is going on and why. Teacher Kelly Cavanaugh had a good activity for defense mechanisms, in *Teaching Tips for General Psychology*. She has her students watch an episode of *Frasier* called *Frasier's Edge,* season 8, episode 12. If you find it on Netflix or Youtube, you can play it and students can identify when the main character, Frasier, a psychiatrist who has a midlife crisis, invokes the defense mechanisms. This takes 20 min, and students like seeing the last moment in human history before cell phones became ubiquitous and instant communication the norm. Crash Course Psychology episode #21.

WEEK 21, MODULES 57, 58, 59: This is the chapter of surveys and personality inventories. Students can take any you choose, and then examine and compare results, and hopefully plot them somehow on a continuum or chart. Bolt's binder has at least 20. Others are online, like the Social Styles inventory, featuring driver, expressive, amiable and social, used by businesses for the last couple decades. You might also have them do the Gregorc Mind Styles inventory. OCEAN spectrum inventories like the BFI are effective and engaging this week, as are clips of stereotypical personalities and type A, type B behavior. View the Ted Talks on introverts by Susan Cain. Crash Course Psychology episode #22.

WEEK 22, MODULES 60, 61: If doing an actual IQ test, the Wechsler is a good choice because it is for adults. Debating the effectiveness of standardized testing as an indicator of future success in college, or for comparison with others or for a job is a good idea. Testing the Sternberg creative and practical intelligences is effective too, as is testing the Gardner multiple intelligences and taking emotional intelligence surveys. The WWI Intelligence Test is humorous, and the Culture-Fair Intelligence test is eye-opening. *Forrest Gump* shows us that high I.Q. doesn't necessarily mean happy, in its portrayal of an intellectually disabled man whose innocence and naivety in a tough world is heartwarming. Crash Course Psychology episode #23. Psychsim Lab: Get Smart.

WEEK 23, MODULES 62, 63, 64: Do the Griggs "One-Minute Intelligence Test." Telling students about MENSA and giving them a MENSA admissions test is possible this week. They are usually intrigued by a society for 'the highly intelligent,' and like seeing videos of MENSA gatherings across the world. This is also a good counterbalance to the thorny issue of group differences in intelligence that appears at this point, highlighted in many politically incorrect but difficult to dismiss articles on the Internet, notably by La Griffe du Lion, an anonymous statistician, at http://lagriffedulion.f2s.com/. If you want to cause controversy, you could present stats from Charles Murray's *Human Accomplishment,* a book that found that over 90-percent of the significant figures in all the arts and sciences of the world for the last 2,500 years, were both white and male. As you might imagine, this caused a backlash and could trigger debate in your class as well as to if, how and why. Yale 13 works here. Crash Course episode #24.

WEEK 24, MODULES 65, 66: Bolt's binder has surveys for nearly all of the maladies in this section, including various anxiety disorders. Students can take them and see how they fit among the groups that have taken them. Warn them they are not to self-diagnose with the surveys, so they don't all leave thinking they have an acute case of OCD or PTSD. Discuss a self-made list of various phobias, and be sure to include *nomophobia*, the phobia of being disconnected from one's social network. OCD themes run through *As Good as it Gets, Matchstick Men* and *The Aviator*. PTSD is a theme in *Rambo: First Blood* and *Apocalypse Now*. Crash Course Psychology episodes #28 and 29. Psychsim Lab: Mystery Client.

WEEK 25, MODULES 67, 68, 69: Psychopathy and sociopathic behavior is no happy topic, but looking at actual psychopathic cases might be a good idea, to see how far the range of human mental maladies can stretch. There are enough cases, sadly, that each student may be able to produce a different case study. If you want to watch a movie, then *Rain Man* is appropriate for this chapter as it deals with Savant Syndrome. *Fight Club* deals with Dissociative Identity Disorder and insomnia. In *Miracle on 34th Street,* a man who believes he is Santa Claus brings Christmas cheer to some New Yorkers in the 1940s. He is promptly sent to a psychologist who says he is delusional. In *Zoolander* and *Mean Girls,* people suffer from narcissistic personality disorder. Many of the villains from the 25+ James Bond movies are good examples of antisocial personality disorder, as is Hannibal Lecter in *Silence of the Lambs. Hamlet,* in any of its incarnations, is a good example of Major Depressive Disorder. Beethoven's story in *Immortal Beloved* may count for bi-polar disorder, its up to you. The *Star Trek* episode *The Conscience of the King* brings up issues of antisocial personality disorder. Yale 18 fits here. Crash Course Psychology episodes #30, 31, 32, and 34. Psychsim: Losing Touch with Reality.

WEEK 26, MODULES 70, 71, 72: Psychotherapy. Get a Ted Talks with Philip Zimbardo called "The Demise of Guys." This wonders how to use therapy to treat video game / dirty movies addiction in males that may be interfering with their social lives and making them depressed (not to mention girls unhappy). You might follow it with an Internet or social network addiction survey. A humorous movie called *Anger Management* looks at group therapy, and *One Flew Over the Cuckoo's Nest* shows institutionalization. Yale episode 19 fits here. Crash Course Psychology episode #35. Psychsim Lab: Computer Therapist (tell students it's a real person on the other end and see how long it takes them to figure out they are not instant messaging).

WEEK 27, MODULES 73: Biomedical therapy is controversial in some cases. Watch the Frontline episode *The Medicated Child*, read Theodore Dalrymple's articles *An Ill for Every Pill* and *Forced Smiles* about Prozac. On the other hand, watch the movie *A Beautiful Mind* to see the wonders and pitfalls of biomedical therapies like Thorazine for schizophrenia, a malady that can hardly be treated without a biomedical intervention. Review the plot of the book *Brave New World,* where a drug called Soma, something like Xanax mixed with Prozac, is used to keep everyone docile, content and… obedient. *Breaking Bad* is a TV series about a high school chemistry teacher whose environment and circumstances change, helping turn him into a producer of crystal meth as he struggles with reconciling his humanity with an emerging antisocial personality disorder, while *Dexter* is a TV series about a sympathetic serial killer. Yale episode 20 works here. Crash Course episode #36. Psychsim Lab: Mystery Therapist.

WEEK 28, MODULES 74, 75: Social Psych material abounds. You'll want to show clips of Asch's conformity experiment, Milgram's obedience experiment, and Zimbardo's prison experiment, all on Youtube. Yale episode 16 works here. Crash Course Psychology episodes #37 and 38. Psychsim Lab: Everybody's Doing It and Social Decision Making.

WEEK 29, MODULES 76, 77, 78, 79, 80: If you want to extend the conformity, obedience, role adoption theme, you can hit Jane Elliott's *Brown Eyes, Blue Eyes* experiment from the 1960s, and then watch the Youtube clip *How Racist are You Elliott* to see the modern application of the technique in Britain. You can also watch *The Wave* (search Youtube: the Wave school experiment). If you are done with the year and the exam is over, you can buy the subtitled German version of the experiment, called *Die Welle,* from Amazon and compare it to both the American version and the actual case. You might look at cooperation and altruism through the lens of Game Theory, as well as present the Prisoner's Dilemma. For love, one can take the Love Styles Quiz online. One may also take any number of Social Attitudes quizzes or prejudice or tolerance inventories. If you want to watch another movie for this material, *Lord of the Flies* fits the bill, covering role assumption, aggression and prejudice, while finding the meaning in life and happiness is the theme in *Dead Poets' Society*. Crash Course Psychology episodes #39 and 40. Psychsim Lab: Dating and Mating, and Not My Type.

Part I

"Manic Monday" and

"Textbook Tuesday"

Class Assignments

Socrates and Plato _____

Aristotle _____

Rene Descartes _____

Francis Bacon _____

John Locke _____

Tabula rasa _____

Empiricism _____

Wilhelm Wundt _____

Structuralism _____

Introspection _____

Functionalism _____

Edward Titchener _____

William James _____

Calkins vs. Washburn _____

Experimental psychologists _____

Sigmund Freud _____

Psychoanalysis _____

Watson and Rayner _____

B.F. Skinner _____

Behaviorism _____

Rogers and Maslow _____

Humanistic psychology _____

Cognitive Neuroscience _____

These philosophers believed mind and body were the same thing:

_____

These philosophers believed mind and body were different things:

_____

Bacon and Locke's ideas helped delineate the norms for the scientific attitude called _____

Wundt and Titchener are to _____ as William James is to _____.

_____ was denied a Harvard degree but _____ was recognized as the first female psychologist for writing *The Animal Mind*.

Pavlov's results helped kick off this school of psychology: _____

Behaviorists believe psychology's definition should be:_____

Give an example of a conclusion they reached _____

Humanistic psychology focuses on the environment around a person too, but emphasizes how that person can overcome their environment.   *a. True*   *b. False*

What did the cognitive revolution turn the focus to? _____

How has cognitive neuroscience contributed to our understanding of psychology?

_____

...and what is, today, the "official" definition of psychology, after we've been studying it for 150 years?

_____

Pg. 8. Congrats! You've finished Module 1. Only 84 left to go. Next step is to read the *Review*, self-evaluate to be sure you are on track, and answer the MC questions 1-5 by weaving the answer into the question in the form of a statement of fact, as in the example below:

1.   *C*   *Wilhelm Wundt established the first psychology lab.*

2

3

4

5

(As per your teacher's instructions, answer the practice FRQs on the back or on a separate sheet).

Nature-Nurture issue

Charles Darwin

Natural Selection

Levels of analysis

Biopsychosocial approach

Behavioral psychology

Biological psychology

Cognitive psychology

Evolutionary psychology

Psychodynamic psychology

Social-cultural psychology

Psychometrics

Basic vs. applied research

Developmental psychology

Educational psychology

Personality psychology

Social psychology

I/O psychology / human factors

Counseling vs. clinical

Psychiatry

Positive psychology

Community psychology

Dorothea Dix

Ready to get de-natured?

Describe the nature-nurture issue:

Today what does the nature-nurture argument 'dissolve' into, as in, what is a good way to think about it:

According to Darwin, how does evolution by natural selection influence the nature-nurture debate?

What does the statement *'nurture works on what nature endows'* mean?

Draw the 3-levels of analysis "biopsychosocial" chart on pg. 11:

Note the kinds of questions the following varieties of psychologists are most interested in:

Behavioral psychologists: *Biological psychologists:*

Cognitive psychologists: *Evolutionary psychologists:*

Humanistic psychologists: *Psychodynamic psychologists:*

Social-cultural psychologists: *Clinical psychologists focus on:*

Do the 5 MC questions on pg. 18. Yes, you should continue to write the answer as a statement.

1

2

3

4

5

Provide examples of what one does in each subfield:

Forensic psychologist

Health psychologist

I/O psychologist

Neuropsychologist

Rehabilitation psych

School psychologists

Sports psychologists

Clinical psychologist

Counseling psychologist

APA

G. Stanley Hall

There are 16 kinds of psychological specialization that people tend to aspire to as a real life occupation. No, you won't find 'introspection therapy' among them, sadly, but you do find a wide-range of different jobs. List the 16 on the left, but in the center, don't define it like on the vocab. Instead, summarize the kinds of things this person does *on the job.* And on the right, rate 1-3 this particular job compared with the others-no right or wrong answers. 3=yeah that's interesting, 2=not bad, and 1=sorry, not very interesting.

SPECIALIZATION	EXAMPLE OF WHAT THEY DO	RATING
1		
2		
3		
4		
5		
6		
7		
8		
9		
10		
11		
12		
13		
14		
15		
16		

Pg. 25. Complete 1-5.

1

2

3

4

5

Hindsight bias
_____

Overconfidence
_____

'Order' in random events
_____

James the Amazing Randi
_____

Critical thinking
_____

Humility
_____

Curious skepticism
_____

By using N.O., S, C.S., E&C groups, and then expressing your findings, you become the Zen research master

What did novelist Madeline L'Engle cite as the three ways we tend to fool ourselves?

_____

_____

What was her conclusion? _____

List some examples of hindsight bias, the "I totally knew that!" phenomenon, at work. Then cite a time someone you know fell victim to hindsight bias (not when you did, cause you *never* would fall into that trap now would you):

_____

You pick- who has the best quote on hindsight bias (circle one): Proverbs, Soren Kierkegaard, Sherlock Holmes, Niels Bohr or Yogi Berra?

Give an example of overconfidence: _____

"With a large enough sample, any outrageous thing is likely to happen." Is this a good explanation why there is so much weird stuff in the world- because our population is now almost 8 billion?___

At the end of the Middle Ages in the late-1200s, Thomas Aquinas argued that if God created the visible universe around us, he would be pleased if we explored the phenomena of nature scientifically. Therefore, it was the responsibility of all good Christians to investigate the world around us. Whose quote on Pg. 35 fits best with Aquinas?

_____

Think of a time you or someone else didn't use critical thinking and made a mistake.

_____

Pg. 37. Complete the MC questions

1

2

3

4

Theory _____

Hypothesis _____

Operation definition _____

Replication _____

Case study _____

Naturalistic observation _____

Survey _____

Population _____

Sampling bias _____

Random sample _____

Representative sample _____

Framing a question _____

Descriptive/correlational/experimental _____

"I'm not a creeper... just doin' a little naturalistic observation"

How is a theory different than a hypothesis? _____

_____

_____

Draw out the scientific method like in the pic on 39, with *you* as the person:

_____

List 3 situations, from the book and/or from your brain, of when case studies are the way to go:

1   *2*   *3*

_____

List 3 situations, from the book and/or from your brain, of when surveys are the way to go:

1   *2*   *3*

_____

List 3 situations when naturalistic observation is the way to go:

1   *2*   *3*

_____

Explain why the larger the sample, the more reliable the results:

_____

Give an example of bad wording on a survey:

_____

How does random assignment minimize bad data? _____

On another page, do the 7 MC questions and the FRQs.

Correlation _____

Correlation coefficient _____

Scatterplot _____

Perfect positive correlation _____

No relationship _____

Perfect negative correlation _____

Correlation vs. causation _____

Illusory correlation _____

Experiment _____

Experimental group _____

Control group _____

Random assignment _____

Double-blind procedure _____

Placebo _____

Independent variable _____

Dependent variable _____

Confounding variable _____

Validity _____

Reliability _____

Strengths (descriptive) _____

Strengths (correlational) _____

Strengths (experimental) _____

There is a correlation between efficiency and lack of redundancy

What's the range of possible correlation coefficients? _____

If there is a perfect positive correlation, describe the line as it appears on the scatterplot:

_____

Describe how the scatterplot looks if there is no relationship between the variables

_____

In which case is there a weaker correlation,

.2 or -.4? _____. Why? _____

What is the *best* example Myers gives to warn us "correlation does not *prove* causation?"

_____

Give an example of an illusory correlation and speculate on why it was an illusion:

_____

_____

Note the 'point to remember' about the difference between a correlational study and an experiment:

_____

What is a good example of a placebo? _____. Which group gets it? _____.

What is the placebo effect? _____

Which group gets the actual treatment? _____

What was the independent variable in the landlord/apartment experiment?_____

What was the dependent variable? _____

The comic on 54 is showing a "reverse placebo effect." Do you: *a. Agree*   *b. Disagree*

If OCD, PTSD and bi-polar disorder were on the next text, and you didn't study that yet, what

would the test *not* be_____. If there were two versions of the test and both were

rather radically different, and you'd have gotten a higher or lower score depending on if you took

"test A" or "test B", then what would the test *not* have? _____.

Ok, there's a high correlation between doing well on the little practice questions and on the next test, the next unit test, and the AP exam. James Randi (aka Bad Santa) said so.

Descriptive statistics

Histogram

'Big, round, undocumented numbers'

Mean

Median

Mode

Measures of central tendency

Skewed distribution

Range

Standard deviation

Normal (bell) curve

Inferential statistics

Observed difference

Statistical significance

Likelihood vs. importance

Get on this assignment... STAT!

How relieved are you (1-10) by the AP Exam Tip box on 56? _____

Mean, median and mode are all _____

In the truck graph on 57, the ironic part about both graphs is that _____

If Trump moved to your town with his 10 billion dollars, would it affect most (and totally skew)

the *a. mean, b. median* or *c. mode* of per capita income in your town? _____

_____ can be thought of as the average distance away from the average, or else, how much individual scores diverge from the mean score.

In the example of the quiz scores, why does knowing standard deviation tell us much more about the quiz and how students did than just knowing the average score?

_____

Under what conditions is an observed statistic considered to be reliable?

1

2

3

"Four out of five dentists recommend Crestgate Quintuple Flouride toothpaste with Gleam Master." How might the company have abused statistics to make this statement?

_____

The "point to remember" for statistical significance is:

_____

Compete the 5 MC questions:

1

2

3

4

5

You may now move on to the FRQ practices on another leaf of paper... STAT! Oh what, that was already used as a cheesy joke? Now that's reliable.

General principles
_____

Specific findings
_____

Culture and Attitude
_____

Ethics
_____

Informed consent
_____

Debriefing
_____

If an experiment's purpose is *not* to re-create exactly behaviors in everyday life, then what is the purpose of an experiment?

_____

Why is there no guarantee that the findings of an experiment will apply to a given individual?

_____

...yet we trust that certain experiments have value. Why? What do they help us describe?

_____

Define culture: _____

Are psychological principles that were theorized and tested by Western people, on Western

populations, necessarily going to be applicable universally in all parts of the world? _____

Pg. 66. Do you think Dave Barry is likely to be a big gambler? _____
(Do you think Kenny Rogers is likely to be a big gambler? Youtube: The Gambler Kenny Rogers)

Is it nice to use animals in psych experiments? _____. Even so, how do researchers who defend the use of animals argue their side?

_____

Circle any of the following you would say should **not** be used in experiments:

Flea   fly   puppy   beetle   cow   chimp   kitten   venus fly trap

Would you have stopped Louis Pasteur's experiment? _____

Who would benefit if you did? _____. Who would suffer? _____

Cite the four regulations concerning experiments on people:

1

2

3

4

Do the 4 review questions (remember: write out the answer in the form of a statement!!! A couple of you have not been doing that, and it shows).

Biological psychology _____

Franz Gall / Phrenology _____

Neuron _____

Dendrite _____

Axon _____

Cell body _____

Myelin sheath _____

Multiple sclerosis _____

Action vs. resting potential _____

Neural impulse _____

Sodium-potassium pump _____

Ions _____

'Selectively permeable' _____

Depolarization _____

Threshold _____

All-or-nothing response _____

Synapse/synaptic gap _____

Neurotransmitters _____

Reuptake _____

Neurotransmitter pathway _____

Common neurotransmitters (6) _____

Endorphins _____

Agonist vs. antagonist _____

Wait so you're what makes up the Internet in my brain? Gee thanks neurons! Zap! Just got another synaptic connection!

Is the comic on 76 true? _____ Why? _____

Although phrenology is debunked, what similarity is there to in phrenology to the modern understanding of the brain?

_____

Everything _____ is simultaneously _____. Summarize the five points we know about the biology of the mind:

1   *2*

3   *4*   *5*

    ---On the back of this or on a separate sheet if you have not done so already, draw a neuron---

Describe the process of depolarization: _____
Draw the sodium/potassium pump:

Why do they call it an all or none response? _____

What did Charles Sherrington discover? _____

How did Santiago Ramon y Cajal describe it _____

What flows through the synaptic gap to the next dendrites? _____
Draw the process happening on pg. 81:

Neurotransmitter	Function	Examples of malfunctions
1		
2		
3		
4		
5		
6		

Answer MC 1-8 and the FRQs

Nervous system _____

CNS vs. PNS _____

Nerves _____

Sensory (afferent) neurons _____

Motor (afferent) neurons _____

Interneurons _____

Somatic nervous system _____

Autonomic nervous system _____

Sympathetic nervous system _____

Parasympathetic nervous system _____

Neural network _____

Reflex _____

Endocrine system _____

Hormones _____

Pituitary gland _____

Adrenal glands _____

Pancreas _____

Testis vs. Ovary _____

Thyroid gland _____

Epinephrine _____

Norepinephrine _____

Fight-or-flight response _____

Secret vocab word: _____

I'm nervous that my endocrine system is pumping out too much adrenalin and making me nervous

Prologue. Huh? Yeah. Before we start, go back to pg. 82 and figure out what an endorphin is:

_____

Think of some examples when endorphins protect us from too much pain:

_____   _____   _____

When a drug gets into your system, it can act as an agonist, meaning:

_____

Or, it may act as an antagonist, meaning:

_____

What do some South American tribes use to paralyze their enemies? _____

Draw the nervous system chart on pg. 87:

What is the human version of what the comic on 88 is telling the bread? _____.

We have _____ neurons, each having roughly _____ contacts w/ other, and

_____ synapses, which are _____.

The human neural net is really like an "Internet in the mind". Agree or disagree: _____
Analyze the reflex chart on 89. Explain why a reflex action is so fast:

_____

Endorphins travel in the _____ system, while hormones are secreted in the _____

How are endorphins and hormones similar? _____

Draw the dude/dudette on 90, sideways, and label the endocrine system's 7 (or 8) different parts:

Lesion _____

EEG scan _____

CT scan _____

PET scan _____

MRI scan _____

fMRI scan _____

Brain stem _____

Medulla _____

Thalamus _____

Reticular formation _____

Pons _____

Cerebellum _____

Limbic system _____

Amygdala _____

Hypothalamus _____

Hippocampus _____

Spinal cord _____

Electrode _____

Pleasure centers _____

Olds and Milner _____

Reward deficiency syndrome _____

11 - THE OLD BRAIN Name_____

You are about to get your head examined

If Sherlock Holmes told you the quote on pg. 94, what would you say to him? _____

What does an EEG do? _____

How does a CT scan work? _____

How does a PET scan work? _____

How does an MRI work? _____

What does an fMRI give us the ability to do? _____

What does the medulla do? _____

What does the pons do? _____

What happened when Magoun cut the cat's reticular formation? _____

What is something a soccer player's cerebellum allows them to do? _____

Do we have to consciously direct our older brain parts to do their work? _____

What happened when Kluver and Bucy lesioned a monkey's amygdala? _____

What did the cat do when they messed with its amygdala? _____

Check the AP Tip on the hypothalamus

What does the hypothalamus monitor? _____.
When you perversely think about mating, or about psychology, describe the process by which you become aroused:

_____

Describe the test subject and the findings of the Olds and Milner experiment:

_____

Well, maybe you are not so perverted after all. Eating, drinking and sex are essential for _____
so, if no one ever thought about them, we would disappear from the face of existence. Still, chill out w/ that.

What neurotransmitter was found to be associated with pleasure? _____

Q. What is reward deficiency syndrome? _____
(or when you haven't gotten the chance to do enough psych homework.) (You know its true.) (MC Time :)

1   *5*

2   *6*

3   *7*

4   *8*

Cerebral cortex _____

'Higher brain' _____

Glial cells _____

Frontal lobes _____

Motor cortex _____

Parietal lobes _____

Somato(sensory) cortex _____

Temporal lobes _____

Auditory cortex _____

Occipital lobes _____

Visual cortex _____

Hemispheres _____

Association areas _____

Phinias Gage _____

Neuroplasticity _____

Neurogenesis _____

Cognitive neural prosthetics _____

'Mind over matter' _____

Broca's Area _____

Paul Broca _____

Carl Wernicke _____

Wernicke's Area _____

Whatever you do, do NOT Youtube: 'Khan Checkov Ear.'

The cerebrum stretched out is about the size of _____. Yum! It has _____ nerve cells.

Why are glial cells called "worker bees?" _____

How do they do that? _____

The researchers who figured out where the particular locations of motor functions in the motor

cortex are, as seen in the rather disturbing diagram on 106, were _____ and_____

The left sensory cortex in the left hemisphere of the parietal lobe senses the _____ side of ze body

You are a lawyer trying to persuade a jury "You have eyes in the back of your head." What do you
say:

_____

When schizophrenics who hear voices that are not there have an MRI done while the voices are
"present," what does the scan show?

_____

So, are they or are they not "hearing" voices? _____

What are association areas? _____
What brain area is involved in language processing?   In speaking?

_____   _____

Provide two example of neural plasticity:

1)   2)

When are our brains most plastic? _____. What are some useful natural
promoters of neurogenesis?Time for some MC questions and FRQs:

1

2

3

4

5

6

_____

Right vs. Left brain

_____

Corpus callosum

_____

Split brain

_____

Roger Sperry

_____

Michael Gazzaniga

_____

Vogel and Bogen

_____

HE.ART

_____

Right brain traits

_____

Left brain traits

_____

Consciousness

_____

Cognitive neuroscience

_____

Dual processing

_____

Handedness

_____

Oh what, you didn't wake up thinking you'd be studying that today? Guess you get to wake up twice today.

What is the corpus callosum's job, and knowing that, do we have 4 brain lobes or 8?

_____

What did Vogel and Bogen discover?

_____

What did Michael Gazzaniga discover in his split-brain research?

_____

Pg. 116 (don't cheat). Draw below what the split brain person is drawing at the same time:

_____

(the result of this constitutes 100% of your grade this marking period and a free 5 on the AP test)

Some left brain strengths: some right brain strengths:

Pg. 118. Read the box 'Handedness.' What percentage of us are right handed? _____.
Is it okay to be left-handed? (give evidence of why or why not):

_____

_____

Is there any REAL evidence for dual processing? Seriously? Is there? Describe it... if it exists:

_____

MC Tyme: your new DJ name.

1   *3*

2   *4*

Behavior genetics

_____

Environment

_____

Chromosomes

_____

DNA

_____

Genes

_____

Genome

_____

Identical twins

_____

Fraternal twins

_____

Twin studies

_____

Separated twins

_____

Thomas Bouchard

_____

Genetic vs. Biological relatives

_____

Molecular genetics

_____

Heritability

_____

Individual differences

_____

Group differences debate

_____

Gene-environment interaction

_____

Epigenetics

_____

Genetic mark

_____

Does good and bad behavior really come from what kind of jeans you have?

Baby pic! Aww… now at what step of the way do nature and nurture work together to shape us? _____

No matter our ethnic background or what culture we embody, we fear strangers at _____

As adults, we: _____
What might a visitor from outer space observe no matter where their flying saucer landed?

_____

Is Jaden Agassi more likely to be a good tennis player if given the opportunity? _____

State the vocab words in 14.1 from littlest to biggest: →   →

When a gene is turned on, what does it do to express itself in the physical world? _____

What accomplishment in genetics did Dr. Francis Collins lead us to? _____
If one twin separated from the other at 2 months is 2 in. taller, what might we conclude as to why?

_____

Can you have male and female identical twins? Why or why not?

_____

What can we conclude about nature and nurture from the story of Jim Lewis and Jim Springer,
who were wombmates but not roommates? (don't forget to check the footnote!)

_____

In general, are adopted kids more like their adoptive or biological parents in the studies done? ___
What is so stunning about this finding?

_____

If you have a bro or sis, do you agree with Steven Pinker when he
says sibling personalities develop in relation to each other, and "ricochet" off each other? _____

Can you think of a time when your mom said, "Your _____ is so _____ and you

are so _____… or… you are the _____ of the family." If yes, do you think

you became more like that characteristic because you were 'expected' to be like that? _____
You can't change the genetic "leash," but how do parents and family home affect kids?

_____

Define heritability: _____

What is the heritability of intelligence? _____. Physical height? _____.

Would you think the comic on 128 was funny if it happened to your future spouse? _____

Evolutionary psychologist
_____

Natural selection
_____

Mutation
_____

Adaptation
_____

Fitness
_____

Steven Pinker
_____

Universal moral grammar theory
_____

Male mating preferences
_____

Female mating preferences
_____

Biopsychosocial: individual development
_____

Science-Faith dialogue
_____

Holistic system
_____

Are good grades a product of natural or artificial selection?

Is Richard Dawkins a Darwin fan?   *Y*   *N*   Are you?   *Y*   *N*

What are the 4 principles of Darwinian evolution theory:

1

2

3

4

The engine of evolution is natural selection, powered by mutation, which is (circle one):

          awesome X-man powers ☺   random errors in gene replication ☹

Are most mutations beneficial or harmful to the organism that is mutated? _____

What is the organism more likely to do if it happens to be beneficial? _____

How do taste buds have survival value? _____

How does Galileo ease the fears of people who are worried about the contradiction between faith and science in the FYI box (pg. 137)?

_____

Teen boys are excited by _____ while _____ somethings prefer girls of their own

age and older guys prefer _____ women. Why? Are they just shallow, or is there an evolutionary reason encoded in the genes of males for this?

_____

Red alert! Red alert! Pg. 141 has a biopsychosocial chart!!!!! Quick, copy it here before it disappears into subspace:

_____

Who had the deepest quote in the chapter, Pascal (139), Ashley, Sagan or Gould: _____

MC 1   *MC2*   *MC3*

Sensation vs. Perception _____

Bottom-up processing _____

Top-down processing _____

Selective attention _____

Inattentional blindness _____

Change blindness _____

Cocktail party effect _____

Psychophysics _____

Transduction _____

Absolute threshold _____

Signal detection theory _____

Difference threshold _____

Subliminal vs. supraliminal _____

Priming _____

Weber's Law _____

Sensory adaptation _____

Gustav Fechner _____

Heather Sellers' prosopagnosia caused her to _____ at the restaurant.

Can you see the secret kiss on pg. 152? Where is it_____

In looking at that, did you do top down or bottom up processing? _____

How many bits of info do our five senses take in per *minute?* _____

Where is your nose? _____. Why does Myers have us look at the X on the page? _____

About what % of traffic accidents involve the driver being distracted? _____

In the comic on 153, who is actually being ignored? _____

Have you ever texted while driving?   Y   N   (if you circled Y, turn yourself in after school)

How does the umbrella chick illustrate inattentional blindness? _____

What is the famous example of change blindness? _____

Is psychophysics the coolest science class you ever heard of, or is it something else (equally cool)?

Transduction is one of the most amazing things the human body can do. Describe it:

What did Gustav Fechner theorize about? _____

You can see a candle flame (circle one)   *1   2   23   30*   miles away at night.

What is the absolute threshold for touch? _____

For olfaction (scent)   _____
Ponder this: how could some tricky storeowners use absolute thresholds to drive away young punks while keeping their older customers who actually buy stuff around?

What is the answer to the riddle on pg. 157? _____

In signal detection theory, do we always notice louder sounds over quieter ones? _____

When can signal detection have life-threatening consequences? _____

Provide an example of how subliminal stimuli can *prime* us: _____

How do the subliminal messaging experiments on pg. 122 illustrate the placebo effect?

Do the 5 MCs and FRQ

Perceptual set

Context effects

Extrasensory perception

Parapsychology

Clairvoyance

I perceive a certain strange enjoyment... it is school-related... I will convince myself these senses are right...

Oops, hold up, one last thing from last module. Go back to pg. 158. We can't skip this.

What is the supraliminal message in the pic with the girl reading our psych book? _____

What was the conclusion of the experiment by Greenwald _____

Back to 163. Which do you see first, the young or old woman? _____. That's ageism!

In the comic on 164, how do people's perceptual sets figure into their error in assumption?

_____

Today with Google Earth, GPS and satellite imagery of the entire surface of the earth, stories about bigfoot, yeti, Loch Ness Monster, swamp monsters, dinosaur leftovers etc. are less in the public imagination than they were even in the 1990s, when people were skeptical but at the same time didn't really know. If 100 people all agreed the pic on 164 was the Loch Ness Monster, would you conform to their opinion?   *Y*   *N*   *Maybe*

If you develop a schema for psychology by going through the class, and then you took it again next year, would you be: *more adept*   *less adept*   *the same*

Why did Africans say the window in the comic was a metal box? Use as many vocab words from

the section as you can_____.

What is the true size of the dogs in the picture in relation to each other? _____
More importantly, can you explain why the illusion works?

_____

"There is more to perception than meets the senses"... what evidence from the section might you bring in to bolster this strange claim?

_____

What would James Randi say about ESP? _____
Circle all that you are willing to admit you have experienced:

Seen a ghost   *used psychic ability*   *met a real psychic*   *experienced the supernatural*

Say aliens from another star actually did arrive on earth. Would they be from the realm of the natural or of the supernatural? Why would meeting a space alien be different than meeting a ghost?

_____

Wavelength _____

Visible spectrum _____

Hue _____

Intensity _____

Wave amplitude _____

Cornea _____

Iris vs. pupil _____

Lens _____

Retina _____

Rods and cones _____

Blind spot _____

Accommodation _____

Optic nerve _____

Fovea _____

Bipolar vs. ganglion cells _____

Feature detectors _____

Parallel processing _____

Face recognition area _____

Motion/form/depth/color _____

Young-Helmholtz theory _____

Opponent-Process theory _____

Afterimage _____

See why this is important?

Remember what *transduce* meant a couple modules ago? _____. If not, review it again.

What is it in one word: _____. Our eyes receive _____ and transduce it

into _____. What actually strikes our eyes? _____.
Draw the spectrum from gamma rays to radio waves. Use crayons if you'd like (and ask for x credit!)

What can bees see that we can't? _____.

If _____ determines the hue of a light-wave, _____determines its brightness.

How is the fovea different from the blind spot: _____

What is (visual) accommodation? _____

Do the dot exercise on pg. 174. Did you find your blind spot? _____.

Why are we more likely to see fuzzy lines in dim light? _____
Speculate on why astronomers in the park using their telescopes get angry when drivers pass by with their lights on?

List two reasons kitty cats see better in the dark than we do:

_____   _____

Do the eye pressure (careful!) exercise on 175. What did you "see" _____

How does parallel processing apply to vision: _____
If you fell in love with someone, and said: "Oh cupcake/button/pumpkin/sweetie/sugar/skittle, you're just oh so beautiful!"; could that person conceivably say back to you: "Is it really me you think is beautiful, or is it the transduced electrical impulses that your visual cortex reconstructs into a meaningful image with its feature detectors, processing my color, motion, form and depth into something your brain recognizes and associates with a positive cluster of memories?"   (Feel free to use in future).
                                                    _____.
If no one sees the tomato, is it red? _____. Why? _____.

How many crayons would you need if you had *all* the colors we can perceptibly differentiate? ____

Can you see something in fig. 18.11? _____. What is it? _____.

What is color blindness... actually? _____

What do fuzzy little puppies see? _____

How is the Young-Hemholtz theory different than the opponent process theory, and what is the present state of understanding about these theories:

Gestalt _____

Necker Cube _____

Figure-ground _____

Grouping _____

Proximity _____

Continuity _____

Closure _____

Depth perception _____

Visual cliff _____

Gibson and Walk _____

Binocular cues _____

Retinal disparity _____

Monocular cues _____

Relative height _____

Relative size _____

Relative motion _____

Interposition _____

Linear perspective _____

Light and shadow _____

Perceptual constancy _____

Color constancy _____

Shape constancy _____

Perceptual adaptation _____

Figure this- you're grounded until you finish every last one of these

What do people tend to see when they look at the Necker cube? _____

Why is the Necker cube a good example of a *gestalt?*

_____

Draw the examples for proximity, continuity and closure, and please label them appropriately:

_____

How did the results of the visual cliff experiment by _____ and _____ change our understanding of depth perception in little humans?

_____

*no matter what, don't ask your teacher to see the Saturday Night Live clip "Mr. No Depth Perception" in the last 5 min. of class.

Do the floating hot dog thing. What psych principle does it illustrate? _____

Okay be creative now. After looking at the six examples on pg. 186, sketch six of your own:

_____

What does the cube with the blue discs tell us about our perception of color?

_____

MC Questions:

1

2

3

4

5

Audition _____

Sound wave amplitude _____

Sound wave length _____

Frequency _____

Pitch _____

Middle ear _____

Inner ear _____

Eardrum _____

Hammer/anvil/stirrup _____

Cochlea _____

Hair cells _____

Cilia _____

Auditory nerve _____

Sensorneural hearing loss _____

Conduction hearing loss _____

Cochlear implant _____

Place theory _____

Frequency theory _____

Loudness _____

Sound shadow _____

Tinnitus _____

I heard this section was really interesting so take your headphones out

If you were forced to give up one sense, which would it be? _____

How many words about hearing or being in the presence of can you think of that come from or are related to 'audition':

How did Myers communicate with his grandma after she lost her hearing? _____

Note a good example of *Pitch*:   Of *Frequency*:   Of *Amplitude*:

_____   _____   _____

At right, sketch out and label the ear on pg. 196:

Why are we acutely sensitive to faint
sounds as well as loud, obnoxious ones?

_____

_____

How many decibels is a *normal conversation*: _____ a *whisper*: _____ a *plane*:_____
What does the ear do to transform sound waves into neural messages?

_____

List the purpose of the following parts vital for audition:

1. outer ear: *2. Auditory canal:*

3. Eardrum: *4. Middle ear (H,A,S):*

5. Cochlea: *6. Basilar Membrane / Hair Cells*

7. Auditory nerve: *8. Thalamus:*

How many hair cells are in a person's cochlea? _____. Where does transduction take place:
What are some risks on pg. 197 to avoid:

How do we *perceive* loudness? _____

Describe Place Theory: Describe Frequency Theory:

How many times can a neuron fire per second:

What happens if the pitch is above that? _____

Why are two ears better than one? _____

Touch _____

Pain _____

Nociceptors _____

Gate-Control Theory _____

Endorphins _____

Pressure/warmth/cold/pain _____

Pain circuit _____

Taste buds _____

Survival value: sweet _____

Survival value: salt _____

Survival value: sour _____

Survival value: bitter _____

Survival value: umami _____

Olfaction _____

Olfactory nerve _____

Kinesthesia _____

Vestibular sense _____

Sensory interaction _____

Embodied cognition _____

Hope your gate-control system is working, you're gonna need it

Dave Barry said the purpose of skin is:

Reproduce the four weird truths about our sense of touch, where each sensation we feel is a variation on pressure, warmth, cold and pain:

1   2

3   4

Honestly, how many of these did you 1) know about, and 2) have personal experience with _____
Why is pain 'a gift' in the opinion of Ashley's doctor?

The point to remember at the bottom of 204. If you think that is a stretch, try to think of a song you like. Play it in your head. Still think you need to be hearing the music to perceive it? _____

Red Alert! Red Alert! Hear the klaxon sound in your head? Its playing because there's a biopsychosocial chart on 205! Quick, copy it:

---

*Don't look up the lyrics to Alice Cooper's song *Poison* and try to say something like, "we should listen to it because it 'goes with this module."

Draw the 'Pain circuit' on 204...   ...and the olfactory sense on 208

Define kinesthesis: What is the vestibular sense?

MC Questions:

1   2

3   4

feel like doing an FRQ?

Consciousness _____

Hypnosis _____

Posthypnotic suggestion _____

Disassociation _____

William James _____

Ernest Hilgard _____

"Dude, is 'Dreamweaver' the coolest song about sleep?" "Nope, 'Silent Lucidity' is." "Really? Never heard of it."

Why didn't Myers have to be 'conscious' to read *Green Eggs and Ham?*

_____

At it's beginning, psychology was the description of _____.

Then in the mid-20th century, this became its focus: _____

Why does Myers say we have a two-track mind? _____

There are many states of consciousness, such as: _____

Check out the AP Exam Tip. How has our understanding of the unconscious mind changed since Freud first hypothesized it a century ago?
          Freud: *Today:*

_____

States that occur spontaneously: _____

States induced physiologically: _____

States induced psychologically: _____

HyPnOsIs Is:

What surprises you most about the facts on hypnosis:

_____

Are there any legitimate uses for hypnosis? How has it been used for the good of the hypnotized individual?

_____

On the other hand, when has hypnosis successfully been used to do harm?

_____

Multiple Choices?

1   3

2   4

Circadian rhythm _____

REM vs. NREM sleep _____

Alpha vs. beta wave _____

EEG _____

Hallucination/hypnagogic sensation _____

Delta wave _____

Sleep paralysis _____

Suprachiasmatic nucleus _____

Pineal gland _____

Melatonin _____

Sleep protects theory _____

Recuperation theory _____

Memory restoration theory _____

Creative thinking theory _____

Growth theory _____

What's your record for not sleeping, measured in total hours awake consecutively? _____

We   *do* / *do not*   process external stimuli when we are asleep.

Do the 5 Question T/F quiz on 225. *1)*   *2)*   *3)*   *4)*   *5)*

Do not look at the answers!!!   Okay now look. How many did you get right? _____

What does circadian mean in Latin? _____ _____. How about *carpe diem?* _____ ____ ____
Though our ancestors had a 24 hr. day, we have more like a 25. Who can we thank for that and why?

NREM sleep takes places in the initial stage _____, and then in _____, _____, and _____,

while REM happens in every 90 min., when the person returns to stage _____.

How many minutes do we dream on an average night? _____. How many min. do you play video

games? _____. During the course of a year, we will have had about _____ dreams, while in

our whole life, we have about _____. What was the topic of your most recent dream:

Describe the role of melatonin in regulating sleep, and which brain parts are active in this:

What is sleep's function? Five theories have been put forth. Summarize their basic premise:

1

2

3

4

5

How long do the following sleep?

bat   cat   cow   dolphin   giraffe   human adult

If you're still awake, complete the MC questions:

1   *3*

2   *4*

Sleep loss
_____

Ghrelin vs. leptin
_____

Sleep disorder
_____

Insomnia
_____

Narcolepsy
_____

Sleep apnea
_____

Night terrors
_____

Sleepwalking
_____

Sleep talking
_____

REM Dream
_____

Daydream
_____

Manifest content
_____

Latent content
_____

Wish fulfillment theory
_____

Information processing theory
_____

Neural pathway development theory
_____

Neural static theory
_____

Cognitive development theory
_____

REM rebound
_____

Nightmare (look it up)
_____

Sigmund Freud
_____

If you commit a crime in a dream, will the dream police come when you wake up?

If you sleep for 5 hours per night for a week, can you sleep for 10 hours to make up for it on Sunday? Why or why not?

_____

Is there a correlation between lack of sleep and depression? _____

Take the 15 question T/F quiz on pg. 183:

1   *2*   *3*   *4*   *5*   *6*   *7*

8   *9*   *10*   *11*   *12*   *13*   *14*   *15*

Now grade it according to the directions below. Are you getting enough sleep? _____
(Just wanted to hear you say it).

What is the breakthrough treatment for memory, mood, hunger moderation and increased

immunity? _____! What % of high school students sleep in class? _____

Which is the dangerous daylight savings time? "Fall back" in Oct. or "Spring ahead" in April? _____

Of the for major sleep disorders, which do you think is the worst to have? _____

For people having trouble sleeping, what are the 8 suggestions widely used by professionals?

1   *2*

3   *4*

5   *6*

7   *8*

What are some common things people dream about?

_____

_____

Do you remember significant dreams from your life? What do you recall the storyline was in one of your dreams? i.e.: what were you doing? Circle any of the following:

Flying   *falling*   *running away*   *playing a sport*   *failing*   *grandma's house*

Add others: _____

Do you recall any symbols in your dreams- things that might mean something
else or reflect something causing you happiness/anxiety in your awake life? _____

Psychoactive drug _____

Substance use disorder _____

Tolerance _____

Addition _____

Withdrawal _____

Neuroadaptation _____

Depressants _____

Alcohol _____

Barbituates _____

Alcohol use disorder _____

Opiates _____

Heroin _____

Stimulants _____

Amphetamines _____

Crystal meth _____

E (MDMA) _____

Nicotine _____

Caffeine _____

Cocaine _____

Hallucinogens _____

LSD _____

Marijuana (THC) _____

Near-death experience _____

25 - DRUGS   User Name _____
                    Don't even think about it

What are psychoactive drugs? _____

What role does neuroadaptation have in a habitual alcohol drinker's requirement for more of the substance to experience the same effects as a non-habitual drinker?

_____

When is drug use a disorder? _____
In 2013, the APA revised its risk-assessments based on symptoms of use into four categories:

Impaired Control	*Social Impairment*	*Risky Use*
1	*1*	*1*
2	*2*	*2*
3	*3*	*Drug Action*
4		*1*

In Thinking Critically on 248, what is a negative consequence of the trend   *2*
of classifying everything someone seems to do to much of as 'an addiction'?

_____

What do all three of the categories of drugs _____, _____ & _____ do?

_____

What are depressants? _____

List at least 3: _____, _____ & _____

Alcohol *disinhibits* people, what does this mean? _____

It also slows neural processing, what does this mean? _____

It disrupts memory, how? _____

It reduces self-awareness, what results? _____

It increases user-expectations. So, would you volunteer for the experiment described? _____

Barbiturates are also called _____. What do they mimic? _____

What is a common street drug that is an opiate? _____. What does it do? _____

List three stimulants: _____ _____ _____

What to they 'do': _____

What does crystal meth do? _____

What surprises you most about caffeine:

What surprises you most about nicotine:

When you see Nic, a teen, smoking on the pages of the book, does it persuade you to lite a smoke? _____

How long does it take for the smoked hit of nicotine to travel to the brain and do its thing? _____

On the cocaine graphic, the key is what goes down in figure C. draw figure C below and describe what is happening on the right:

Fig. C: Explanation:

_____

_____

_____

Bee a spelling bee winner! Try to spell the long-form name of ecstasy: _____
(look for 5 seconds then write)

What does ecstasy do to people _____

What are hallucinogens and their effects? _____

What is a near death experience? _____

What is THC? _____

How does marijuana alter a person's consciousness? _____

Uniquely, marijuana flips the regular tolerance pattern. Habitual users actually need less of it to become 'high' then people who do not use it habitually. Why is this so?

Do the MC questions here, and the FRQ on a separate sheet, then you're done! Of course, then you will experience withdrawal. But don't worry. More psych will be on the way!

1   *3*

2   *4*

Learning
_____

Habituation
_____

Learning by association
_____

Stimulus-response
_____

Cognitive learning
_____

Classical conditioning
_____

Ivan Pavlov
_____

His dog
_____

Behaviorism
_____

John Watson
_____

Neutral stimulus
_____

US vs. UR
_____

CS vs. CR
_____

Acquisition
_____

Extinction
_____

Spontaneous recovery
_____

Generalization
_____

Discrimination
_____

Little Albert
_____

Ready... Set... Learn! Well? Learn! Come on now... Learn! Well- at least get conditioned.

Please define learning:_____

You are hereby requested and required to give an example of learning by association:

_____

Because you signed up for this course, you must now explain the story of the sea slug habituating:

_____

In the space provided here at taxpayer expense, describe forthwith how the story of the thunderstorm is a good example of associative learning:

_____

Earn points by revealing which branch of psychologists absolutely loves studying conditioning:

How do we learn in classical conditioning? _____

What has Snoopy 'learned' in the comic on 266? _____

Describe Pavlov's dog experiment in terms of what was the UR, US, CR and CS:

        What is it   Why?

UR:

US:

CR:

CS:

What was acquired in the Pavlov experiment _____

What was extinguished later _____

What was spontaneously recovered after that?_____

What could be added to the Pavlov experiment to make it higher-order conditioning?

_____

Summarize the significant findings of the Little Albert Experiment by Watson and Rayner:

Operant conditioning _____

Edward Thorndike _____

Law of Effect _____

Puzzle box _____

Operant chamber/Skinner box _____

Shaping _____

Reinforcement _____

Successive approximations _____

Discriminative stimulus _____

Positive reinforcement _____

Negative reinforcement _____

Primary vs. secondary reinforcer _____

Reinforcement schedule _____

Fixed ratio schedule _____

Variable ratio schedule _____

Fixed interval schedule _____

Variable interval schedule _____

Continuous reinforcement _____

Partial (intermittent) reinforcement _____

Positive punishment _____

Negative punishment _____

Punishment controversy _____

Aversive vs. rewarding stimulus _____

How is operant conditioning *different* from classical conditioning?

Describe the Thorndike Puzzle Box experiment, from which he theorized the Law of Effect:

Experiment: *Results:*   *Law of Effect:*

Describe the Skinner Pigeon experiment, from which he theorized the principle of conditioning:

Experiment: *Results:*   *Conditioning:*

Reproduce the table 'ways to increase a behavior' on 278.

Term	Description	Example

Should parents always give the baby some reward when they cry? What does Skinner and the comic on 278 say about what might happen if they did?

The mouse on 279 is actually saying something quite funny. Can we generalize this (no pun intended) to mean we all tend to work for rewards? Comment on whether you think we do or if there's more to us than that:

Describe the four schedules of reinforcement:

Positive punishment? Seriously? What did Skinner mean by that?

Applications at school
_____

...in sports
_____

...at work
_____

...at home
_____

...for self-improvement
_____

Amy Sutherland
_____

Biofeedback
_____

Respondent behavior
_____

Operant behavior
_____

So would you rather have some negative reinforcement or some positive punishment?

Do you think textbooks should be replaced with online books, Kindle books, or .pdf files on your phone in all your classes at school? Why or why not?

_____

Would school be better if you had lots of little quizzes, even Kahoot.it style ones online with, say, the MC questions at the end of each module that you could answer on your way out? Or is it better to read at home and do the MC questions there?

_____

What advice would a behaviorist doing operant conditioning give to sports managers?

_____

What about to bosses at work?

_____

After reading the advice of behaviorists to parents, what from it do you see yourself employing to your future hypothetical family?

_____

Would you feel comfortable if you future husband or wife 'trained' you, like Amy Sutherland did her husband in the box 'Close-up' on 288?   *Y*   *N*

Why? _____

The big chart. You like these, right? Its on 290 and its important- lots of info here. Summarize:

ITEM	Classical Conditioning	Operant Conditioning

MC _____

1	3	5
2	4	

John Garcia
_____

Taste aversion
_____

Biological constraints on conditioning
_____

Predictability vs. expectancy
_____

Cognitive map
_____

Latent learning
_____

Insight
_____

Intrinsic vs. extrinsic motivation
_____

Problem-focuses coping
_____

Emotion-focused coping
_____

Learned helplessness
_____

Self-control and long term gratification
_____

Internal vs. external locus of control
_____

Gung-ho behaviorists like Greg Kimble thought in the 1950s that basically every single behavior an animal made was a conditioned response. They thought all behaviors could be shaped into something different. What did they have to admit by the 1980s?

Party Time! Take a quick look at the top of 293. Yeah, you know John Garcia is smiling for a reason- he sees the biopsychosocial chart on learning! Copy the chart, asking for help if you see a term you don't understand in any of the fun colored boxes:

What did John Garcia contribute the study of learning:

Nothing tastes sweeter to a behaviorist than taste aversion therapy. Why? What is done?

How does the color red represent either a conditioned stimulus OR a biological predisposition:

Conditioned stimulus: *biological predisposition:*

Genetic predispositions matter. How did Mark Twain teach us about them in layman's terms:

What's the main principle on how biology (nature) limits the power of environment (nurture):

Describe how the British kids were conditioned using ice cream:

Describe how kids were conditioned using *Pokemon*:

Why does learned helplessness occur?

What does perceived self-control predict, vs. a perceived lack of self-control?

Describe the benefits of an internal locus of control   Your reward: an
(or else, why do people like I-pods and dvr's?):   MC/FRQ area on back

Observational learning _____

Modeling _____

Albert Bandura _____

Bobo doll experiment _____

Vicarious reinforcement _____

Mirror neurons _____

Imitation _____

Theory of mind _____

Prosocial behavior _____

Model caregiver _____

Antisocial effects _____

Media-Violence controversy _____

Robert Rescorla _____

Edward Tolman _____

Violence-viewing effect _____

The line must be drawn here: _____

Does this mean if I cheat off someone's paper, I'm just observing what they learned?

Just think, Albert Bandura let kids beat up a "Bobo doll" balloon and filmed it, and now he gets huge perks, like when he went to DC and the hotel clerk gave him an upgrade. What was the point of the Bobo doll experiment?

What does the term *vicarious* mean in Bandura's extended conclusions about the Bobo doll experiment?

If you have a brother of sister, did they ever 'copy' you and you got mad, and your mom said something like "remember, imitation is the best form of flattery"? What role did your sibling's mirror neurons play in all this?

How important are role models according to Bandura and Joseph Joubert, whose quote is at left?

How is the observed pain- shown in the brain on the right, similar and different to the experienced pain of the brain on the left?

Can you imagine not watching TV for a month?   *Y*   *N*

Say the power went out and you couldn't watch TV or play video games, or use your phone or a computer, and your Kindle or Nook or other reader ran out of batteries. Read the FYI on 308. What do you think you spend the week doing?

The average American kid spends _____ hours watching TV, while the average adult spends_____.

In thinking critically on pg. 309, some examples of the violence-viewing effect are presented. What are they?

How does a statement like "nuclear energy can be used for good, like in power plants, or for ill as in atomic bombs" compare with the statement "prosocial behavior or antisocial behavior can be influenced by observational learning":

Memory _____

Encoding _____

Storage _____

Retrieval _____

Parallel processing _____

Sensory memory _____

Short-term memory _____

Long-term memory _____

Working memory _____

Explicit memory _____

Implicit memory _____

Automatic processing _____

Effortful processing _____

Iconic _____

Echoic _____

Chunking _____

Mnemonics _____

Memory hierarchies _____

Spacing effect _____

Testing effect _____

Shallow processing _____

Deep processing _____

Richard Atkinson: **Richard Shiffrin:**   **George A. Miller:**

31 – MAKING MEMORIES

Something seems eerily familiar about all this

Remember to define memory: _____

What were the humanoids able to do who had previously seen the disconnected lines

in the comic on 318? _____. What do you think it is? _____.

How many single digits could you or I 'parrot back' upon hearing them _____

After seeing 2,500 pictures, what is the average human accuracy in recalling them? _____

Trace the three stages of memorization:

Encoding: _____Storage: _____Retrieval: _____

Provide examples of the following: Sensory memory: _____

Short-term memory: _____; Long-term memory: _____

(and don't forget) Working memory: _____
What does Myers mean by the phrase "sometimes Google replaces rehearsal?"

Your brain does _____ processing while a computer does _____

Give examples of the following, which we automatically process:

Space _____*Time*_____ *Frequency* _____

What's an example of something you'd store in *echoic* memory: _____ *Iconic*: _____

FYI 322: the 7 magic 7s! What is psych's contribution?_____

Give an example of something you've rehearsed recently _____

What have you chunked recently to remember? _____
Take a moment to recall a mnemonic device not in the chapter. What was it:

_____

Yo think about it. How is Wikipedia a good example of hierarchies in action?

Concerning rehearsal, is it better to study   *a) all at once*   *b) in spaced out periods of time*?

We have tests once a week instead of once every two weeks. Why is that good for memory?
If you rehearse the names of people new to you, the serial position effect says you will remember
the (circle one):   *earlier*   *middle*   *later*   names more easily.

Hippocampus (role) _____

Amnesia _____

Basil ganglia (role) _____

Infantile amnesia _____

Amygdala (role) _____

Cerebellum (role) _____

Flashbulb memory _____

LTP _____

Alzheimer's disease _____

Recall _____

Recognition _____

Relearning _____

Rehearsal _____

Priming _____

Mood-congruent memory _____

Context-dependent memory _____

Serial-position effect _____

Recency _____

Primacy _____

Eric Kandel _____

Hermann Ebbinghaus _____

Retrieve Fido, retrieve! Run across the field, and retrieve all my life's memories! What, you don't name your neurons?

Contrast how the brain stores memories vs. how a library stores information (pt. 2 rmbr.)

_____

Contras the role of the hippocampus with the role of the frontal lobes in memory processing:

_____

(If you saw a hippo on campus, you'd remember the hippocampus is involved in memory formation)

Contrast the role of the basil ganglia and the cerebellum in memory storing:

_____

Infantile amnesia erases our memory of being born and living for about 3 years. What kind of

memory, for most people, is their earliest one? _____
What's yours earliest memory? Is it a flashbulb memory of something traumatic or amazing, or is
it crawling around on a certain color carpet that was in your room?

_____

Come up with 3 flashbulb memories for:

YOU_____

SOCIETY_____

Bro, even Myers' AP Exam Tip on 334 says you would benefit amazingly by copying figure 32.5:
So go ahead, we'll wait:

Contrast context and state dependent memory:

_____

Circle: Are you doing **automatic** or **effortful** processing right now as you learn these concepts?

Forgetting
_____

Anterograde amnesia
_____

Retrograde amnesia
_____

Encoding failure
_____

Storage decay
_____

Forgetting curve
_____

Retrieval failure
_____

Proactive interference
_____

Retroactive interference
_____

Repression
_____

Misinformation effect
_____

Imagination inflation
_____

Source amnesia
_____

Déjà vu
_____

Repressed memories court controversy
_____

SQ3R
_____

Rehearsal strategy
_____

Meaningfulness strategy
_____

Retrieval cues strategy
_____

Mnemonic device strategy
_____

Interference minimization
_____

Sleep strategy vs. Testing
_____

Elizabeth Loftus

Read the CS Lewis quote on 342, and imagine the majesty of the observable universe. Anyway what's for lunch?

Jimmie had anterograde amnesia, which means he _____

When Dr. Sacks shoed him a picture of the moon, why did he think it was a picture of earth?

_____

How are Alzheimer's and anterograde amnesia patients similar?

_____

Describe the findings of Ebbinghaus as illustrated by his famous forgetting curve:

_____

(Here's a mnemonic device for Ebbinghaus: he's the dude who showed our memories 'ebbing' away over time! Get it? Ebbing away?)

How many years after high school will it take for most of
the Spanish you learned to evaporate from your memory? _____

Looking at the chart on 346, describe the flow process of how the brain stores our memories:

_____

_____

_____

_____

Eyewitness testimony on the stand in a courtroom is one of the hallmarks of the Western judicial process. If you were a lawyer for the defense and someone pointed out your client as guilty because they 'saw' something, what could you say in refute to get your client off even though they probably did it:

_____

_____

Improving memory: Now for some relevant and worthwhile study of memory improvement techniques:

1

2

3

4

5

6   7

Cognition

Prototype

Concept

Creativity

Convergent vs. divergent thinking

Expertise trait

Imaginative thinking trait

Venturesome personality trait

Intrinsic motivation trait

Creative environment

Think about it. Seriously. Now that's a concept.

Define cognition:

Give three examples of concepts:

_____   _____   _____

What do concepts do for us? _____

Give an example of a prototype: _____

Why is it harder to conceptualize a penguin as a bird than for them to conceptualize a robin? Isn't that just mean? Penguins are birds too you know.

_____

Why should V8 juice actually be F8? _____

Fermat's Last Theorem is a challenge for mathematicians. The Princeton mathematician used

_____ to solve it. Define it further:

Convergent thinking is _____while

Divergent thinking is _____

Creativity is spurred on by 5-factors. Name each and summarize how its influence works:

1

2

3

4

5

Want to be more creative? Well, Myers says you can be. Summarize how:

1

2

3

Heuristic vs. Algorithm _____

Insight _____

Confirmation bias _____

Fixation _____

Mental set _____

Intuition _____

Representative vs. Availability heuristic _____

Overconfidence _____

Fear factor _____

Belief perseverance _____

Framing _____

Wolfgang Kohler: **Amos Tversky:**   **Daniel Kahneman:**

35 – PROBLEM SOLVING   **NAME** _____

Think about it. Seriously. Now that's a concept.

If you went shopping for baking powder, what do you do if you don't know where it is in the store and you are using an algorithm thinking strategy to find it?

_____

What might you do if you are using a heuristic?

_____

How is algorithmic thinking different than solving by trial and error?

_____

An Aha! moment comes when you are trying to solve a problem you are fo-real interested in solving, and the answer jumps into your mind as if from nowhere. The puzzle pieces fit together now…

…and you realize, you just solved a problem by _____.

How is the 2005 Iraq War a good example of confirmation bias?

_____

What is intuition? _____

How do smart thinkers use it? _____

Can you problem-solve and figure out 35.2? In how many seconds? _____

When did you last use a representative heuristic:

What messed up the person's thinking in the poetry example? _____

When did you last use an availability heuristic:

Give an example of the availability heuristic in action:

When were you last overconfident?_____

Give another example: _____

FEAR FACTOR: why was it incorrect, even deadly, to avoid flying because you thought flying was more dangerous than driving long distances?

_____

When did you last have belief perseverance? _____

Give another example: _____

How did the textbook 'frame' the Iraq War earlier in the chapter?

Language _____

Phoneme _____

Morpheme _____

Grammar _____

Babbling stage _____

One-word stage _____

Two-word stage _____

Telegraphic speech _____

Noam Chomsky _____

Universal grammar _____

Aphasia _____

Broca's area _____

Wernicke's area _____

Linguistic determinism _____

Imagination _____

Benjamin Lee Whorf _____

Critical periods _____

Unsymbolized thoughts _____

Steven Pinker _____

Speak Sparky, speak! "Arf, hou hou, woof, bark, errr… ruff ruff!" Sparky… did the noises you made influence the way you think?

Herodotus, the Greek historian who pioneered the field, said that he was fascinated by the fact that writing was a way to keep someone's ideas and thoughts outside of your head. He wrote the history of the Persian-Greek Wars, in which he was a hoplite soldier, to keep the memory alive, and we still read about it today. Compare Herodotus to the rabbi on pg. 372.

_____

_____

Phoneme, phonics, phone, phonograph, phonetic, all relate to _____

Mnemonic device alert! _____ 'morph' units of sound into units of meaning!

What does Noam Chomsky argue all languages in the world have in common _____

What can 7-year olds do that adults have a hard time with? _____

What part of the brain is Broca's area located in vs. Wernicke's area?

_____

How is learning about Broca and Wernicke in this chapter a good example of rehearsal?

_____

Draw the 2nd Try This on pg. 379 here on the right- don't look at the upside down text until you are done!

_____

Think of the grades you have learned a foreign language in. What were the grades, what was the language(s) and how much do you remember? Could you converse with a native speaker of that language?

_____

Now read the 4th paragraph on 380. Would you propose a change in foreign language instruction? How would you recommend your district do it in the future if you were designing the curriculum?

_____

Can you think of images, stills from a scene in your life's past, photographs, places, and imaging being there right now? What images do you think of first?

_____

Do the MC questions and FRQ, and please, use good language while doing so.

Motivation _____

Instinct theory _____

Drive _____

Drive-reduction theory _____

Homeostasis _____

Incentives _____

Optimum arousal theory _____

Curiosity _____

Yerkes-Dodson law _____

Hierarchy of Needs _____

Physiological needs _____

Safety needs _____

Belongingness needs _____

Esteem needs _____

Aesthetic needs _____

Self-actualization needs _____

Self-transcendence needs _____

Abraham Maslow _____

Intrinsic motivation _____

Extrinsic motivation _____

What do you think... should we get started on that motivation research or not?

After sipping his own urine, saying goodbye to his family and passing out in the mountains, what motivated Aaron Ralston to cut off his own arm and repel down a 65 ft. cliff with his other one?

_____

There are three theories of what motivates people. They are called (old name)_____,

(new name) _____, _____, and _____.

What qualifies as an instinct? _____; Example:

What is the goal of our instincts in this theory? _____

What is the aim, or goal, of drive-reduction? _____, which is _____

In D.R. theory, we are pushed by _____ and pulled by _____

Think of an example of an incentive 'pulling' us _____

In optimum arousal theory, what do we do when we are well fed and comfortable?

_____

Why did George Mallory want to climb Mt. Everest? _____

Why don't D.R. and O.A. theory match each other? _____

Copy Maslow's Hierarchy of Needs from 393:

Where are you on Maslow's Hierarchy now?

_____

Where on the hierarchy do you think George
Mallory was while on the peak of Mt. Everest?

_____
Where is someone who gets a gold star for
good work? _____

Where is an Olympic athlete who brought
home a gold medal for his/her fatherland?   _____

Where are you when your friends call and
ask you to hang out doing some fun things?   _____

Where is someone who just got a UN rice pack in the middle of a famine? _____

Ancel Keys _____

Hunger drive _____

Glucose _____

Set point _____

Basal metabolic rate _____

Appetite hormones _____

Cultural preferences in food _____

Ecology of eating _____

Obesity _____

Waist management strategies _____

Ah yes, food. That weird mushy stuff we eat. You are what you eat, aren't you? I mean, elementally speaking?

If you don't think hunger is a big motivator just wait a little while! Same with thirst. What did the semi-starvation experiment of 1950 show happened to the volunteers after they were fed ½ rations for 6 months?

Symptoms _____

How did they express what they became obsessed with?

_____

What was Washburn's stomach doing when he was feeling pangs of hunger? _____

What is the role of glucose in human biology? _____

When glucose is low, what happens? _____

The "I'm hungry" hormone is called _____ and is secreted by your _____.

The "I'm full" hormone is called _____ and is secreted by your _____.

The blood sugar level hormone is called _____ and is secreted by your _____.

The "Hey, stomach's hungry" brain hormone secreted by the hypothalamus is _____.

Semi-starved or over-fed people or animals can get a new _____.

How did the semi-starved volunteers lose only 1/3 of their weight but were eating half of the amount of food they would normally? What else changed?

_____

Why did the tattoo guy on the right get that on his arm? What *motivated* that humorous decision?

_____

How much food will you eat over the next 20 years? _____

Some people who are depressed crave _____ because _____

Sweet and salty food cravings are usually _____but could be _____

What factors predispose some people to become and remain obese?

_____

On the BMI chart, what is a healthy weight for:

    A. 5 ft. 7 person? _____   B. 5 ft. 11 person?_____

Sexual response cycle
_____

Refractory period
_____

Sexual dysfunctions
_____

Testosterone
_____

Estrogen
_____

External stimuli
_____

Imagined stimuli
_____

Masters and Johnson
_____

Well, without it, none of us would ever have been born, humanity would go extinct, and there would be no need to study psychology any further.

So, suppose you walk up to a table where Masters and Johnson are looking for volunteers for a psychology experiment. Cool! You think, and then you ask what the nature of the experiment is and they tell you as Myers writes it on 406. Do you (seriously now) after the initial shock wears off, volunteer or not? Why or why not?

_____ , because _____

In great detail- okay, just kidding- in regular, good old, totally normal, basic level detail, identify the stages in the sexual response cycle:

_____

Is the male or female refractory period longer? _____. Aren't you glad to know that?

Which sex hormone is shared by both males and females in greater degree? _____

Don't get too aroused (emotionally- get your mind out of the gutter) but there is a biopsychosocial chart on 409 to copy!

Do you agree with the cartoonist on 409 (and also the quote below it) that basically our society has been allowed to be taken over by hypersexual advertising and media of every sort? What is your opinion on whether it is true and if it is good, bad or doesn't matter?

_____

_____

What does the viewing of x-rated films tend to do to people's relationships in real life?

_____

How might each of the following theories explain the sexual motivation of human beings?

Evolutionary perspective   Drive reduction theory   Arousal theory

Belonging _____

Affiliation need _____

'Us' and 'them' _____

Insecure anxious attachment _____

Insecure avoidant attachment _____

Ostracism _____

Social networking _____

Narcissism _____

Be careful what you do. Your social network is watching. And reporting.

What does affiliation mean in the context of this chapter?

_____

What are some of the benefits of 'belonging' according to the text?

_____

What seems to be more important than money, if you believe the university study?

_____

What is self-esteem a gauge for? _____

What was the rationale for US immigration officials to begin encouraging chain migration from other countries?

_____

Why is ostracism bad for people?

_____

Do more people in India have a cell phone or a toilet? _____

What percentage of college kids have Facebook or Twitter? _____

Think of some negatives of spending time on social networking site:	To be fair, what is positive about spending time social networking:

Does your online profile, or that of someone you know, reflect the real you (or them)? _____

What does Myers say at the top of 418 about profiles? _____

What is a narcissist and why might they use a social network?

Emotions _____

James-Lange theory _____

Cannon-Bard Theory _____

Schachter-Singer theory _____

Spillover effect _____

Amygdala's role _____

Cognition's role _____

Zajonc and LeDoux theory _____

Lazarus theory _____

Emotional arousal _____

Sympathetic nervous system _____

Parasympathetic nervous system _____

Polygraph test _____

Really? Are we going to do this here?

Read the opening page. Do you think Myers should have his son taken away by Child Protective Services and placed in foster care after learning of this neglect? Circle: Y   N

Myers' emotions swung from terror into ecstasy that day. Now think of a time when your emotions did that- swung rapidly from one kind to another. What happened to trigger it?

_____

Emotions are our body's adaptive response. They are a mix of 1)_____

2) _____ and 3)_____

What is the puzzle in all this?_____

What was William James (1890) view? _____

If you were a player in the picture of the girls' basketball team, which order of events seems to

make the most sense to you, imagining it all going down _____

Give an example that supports the James-Lange Theory:

_____

Now one that supports the Cannon-Bard Theory: _____

And yet another that bolsters the 2-Factor Theory: _____

Conversely, what did Zaonc, LeDoux argue? | How 'bout Lazarus?
                                                    |
_____|_____

425: The _____ division of the _____ mobilizes the body and releases the

stress hormones _____ and _____ when something in the

environment makes us fight or _____. No not that kind of flea.

What does the liver do in such an emergency? _____

When the crisis is over and everything √'s out, what happens? _____

Which film would you volunteer to watch in Myers' experiment on 427? _____

Which brain hemisphere, *left* or *right*, is associated with depression-prone people? _____

Does the guy in the chair on 348 look like he'd lie no matter what the machine says?

'Male' emotions _____

Emotional literacy _____

Gestures _____

Universal expressions (7) _____

Smile therapy _____

Facial feedback _____

Mom the school said I was on an emotional rollercoaster. And FYI, it just flew off its tracks ☺

Why should you be careful with staring contests with the opposite sex? _____

How do graphic novels and comics make it clear to the reader what the people are thinking?

_____

According to the chart on 435, which gender is more expressive? _____

President Nixon ripped Brazilians without knowing it (or did he?) by doing this:

_____

What did the US Navy spies captured by North Korea do? _____

What are Ekman's 6 'universal expressions'? _____

Draw them as if you were drawing them for a comic:

How did Darwin explain expressions? _____

What does it say about the role of biology if Scandinavians and Scandinavian Americans use less rambunctious facial expressions while both Irish and Irish Americans use more?

_____

Draw an example of facial feedback that you have experienced:

_____

MC

1

2

3

_____

Stress _____

Extreme stress _____

Stressors _____

Catastrophe _____

Life change _____

Daily hassles _____

Stress response system _____

GAS _____

Fight or flight _____

Tend-and-befriend _____

Telomere shortening _____

Oxytocin _____

Hans Selye _____

Psychophysiological illness _____

Psychoneuroimmunology _____

Lymphocytes _____

B vs. T lymphocytes _____

Macrophage _____

NK cells _____

HIV _____

AIDS _____

Cancer _____

Carcinogen _____

Coronary heart disease _____

Type A personality _____

Type B personality _____

Pessimism and stress _____

Depression and stress _____

Robert Sapolsky _____

If they ask you to volunteer for them to make a documentary about you and stress reactions, say no.

How would you rate stress in your life, 1 (low) out of 10 (high) _____

Make a list of the stressors from the book:	Now list the stressors in your life:
	|
	|
	|
	|
	|
	|
	|

Describe the stress response system:

_____

Pg. 448. Describe the role of the immune system's lymphocytes (both kinds) and how too much stress affects this system:

_____

_____

_____

_____

Summarize stress and AIDS:	*Summarize stress and Heart Disease:*
Summarize stress and Cancer:	*Summarize pessimism and Heart Disease:*

_____

MC pg. 446	*MC pg. 455*
1	*1*
2	*2*
3	*3*

Nature and development _____

Nurture and development _____

Stability of development _____

Change through development _____

Temperament _____

Conception _____

Zygote _____

Embryo _____

Fetus _____

Placenta _____

Teratogens _____

FAS _____

Rooting reflex _____

Habituation _____

*Usually we say 'violence is not the answer.' But if anyone in your class says 'back when I was in my mom's stomach' instead of womb, well, maybe we can make an exception. Or rather just tell them you **wish** that had been the case!*

What does Myers mean by saying we can see the flow of life as a continuity or by stages on a chart? What examples of stage theories does he give?

_____

In the comic on 463, about what point are you at? _____. How about your teacher?_____

Are you a big smiler like Miss Smiley McNoWayThat'sSoGreat!!! on the right, a medium smiler, or a 'not so much' smiler like Miss AreYouSeriouslyTakingAPictureOfMeRightNow on the left?

_____

What is this dot _ . _ the same size as? _____

How many space voyagers approach that little dot in Darwinian competition? _____

When a single spermatozoa bonds with the egg cell and becomes one with it, that initial cell is a

new human being, as it was you so many years ago. This is called the moment of_____.

Why was this one of your most fortunate moments? _____
(People say they never won anything, but actually, everyone alive did. We all won the most important lottery ever- the lottery of life vs. oblivion)!

If a different one would have gotten in, would 'you' be 'you?' _____
                    Note the relevant characteristics of each stage:

Zygote:

Embryo:

Fetus:

List their timeframes:

_____zygote_____embryo_____fetus_____→

After 38 weeks living 'underwater,' whose voice does the newborn like best? _____

The mothers _____ was screening out _____ which are harmful.

List some things that can't be screened effectively:

1/800 people had FAS as a newborn, why? _____

What is habituation? _____

Maturation
_____

Pruning process
_____

Back-to-sleep position
_____

Infantile amnesia
_____

Motor development
_____

Cognition
_____

Jean Piaget
_____

Schemas
_____

Assimilation
_____

Accommodation
_____

Sensorimotor stage
_____

Preoperational stage
_____

Concrete operational stage
_____

Formal operational stage
_____

Object permanence
_____

Conservation
_____

Symbolic thinking
_____

Egocentrism
_____

Theory of mind
_____

Autism spectrum disorder
_____

Abstract reasoning
_____

Lev Vygotsky
_____

Scaffolding
_____

Whoa, major flashback!

Describe maturation using other words: _____

The _____ gives us motor control, poise and gets us ready to crawl and walk.

What is the recommended way to put a baby to sleep in the crib? _____

Infantile amnesia affects us all, and makes memories before _____ hard to find in our heads.

How do schemas aid our cognition:

How does assimilation aid our cognition:

How does accommodation aid our cognition:

Look at the impossible object in fig. 9.9. What's up with that? _____

PIAGET'S STAGES	DESCRIPTION	DEV. PHENOMENA
1)		
2)		
3)		
4)		

Kids are dumb. What does the girl in 479 not understand? _____

If you were marketing a soda to teenagers and idiots at the gas station, what kind of bottle would you put it in and why?

When kids develop a theory of mind, what can they now do? _____

What mistake does that Roger from the comic make? _____

What is one of the problems researchers find with Piaget's stages? _____

How is Lev Vygotsky's scaffolding theory different than Piaget? Is it also a 'stage theory?'

Stranger anxiety _____

Attachment _____

Harlow Monkey Experiment _____

Critical period _____

Imprinting _____

Konrad Lorenz _____

Mere exposure _____

Temperament _____

"Strange situation" _____

Difficult vs. Easy babies _____

Jerome Kagan _____

Erik Erikson _____

Basic trust _____

Self-concept _____

Authoritarian _____

Permissive (lax) _____

Authoritative _____

Western then vs. Western now _____

Family self _____

Mary Ainsworth _____

Diana Baumrind _____

Don't get too attached to this module

Babies form attachments easily cause they're afraid and ill-equipped to live on their own. Fraidy cat babies! Guess what? They're afraid of strangers too. Describe why you think that might be:

_____

The _____, _____ and _____-_____ behavior develop together.

Imagine you were describing the Harlow monkey experiment to someone who never heard of it and didn't have kids. How would you explain what it told us about attachment?

_____

_____

_____

What happened when the baby monkey was put in a new situation without its 'mother'? _____

Describe the kinds of temperament: _____

Estimate your temperament as a kid: _____

To what extent do you think temperament as a baby predicts character and personality as an older person?

_____

If you see the dude on 491, the guy calling himself a "stay at home dad", do you think he is:

A. Using it as a way to get out of work   *B. Playing a role not suited for him*

C. Leaching off the public welfare system   *D. Married to someone who has a better job than he does*

How does basic trust influence attachment?

_____

The major crisis of babyhood is developing either trust, or distrust of the world around you.

What might cause a baby to develop distrust? _____

Aside from humans above baby-age, what other animals have a 'self-concept?'

_____

Describe the three styles of parenting and estimate which kind your parents had:

Gender identity

Carol Gilligan

Sex (biological identity)

Aggression

Directive vs. democratic

Independent vs. interdependent identity

Gender role

Role

Gender identity

Social learning theory

Gender typing

Gender schema

Transgender

Is this section gendered?

Check out the FYI on 500. What rationale is provided for boys having blue and girls having pink?

_____

Imagine you are a parent. Do you buy pink for boys and blue for girls, or go the traditional route, or does it not matter? And if it does matter, does it matter more for boys or girls? Why?

_____

_____

_____

Summarize the influence of gender on relative levels of aggression:

_____

Contrast directive vs. democratic patterns of interaction with others:

_____

Is one of the pictures on the bottom of 502 showing a scene that the kids are doing something inherently less valuable than in the other scene? If so, which one? And why is it less important?

_____

List some come common stereotyped gender roles that society has for:
  Males   *Females*

_____

Do you consciously recall when and where you developed your *gender schema?* Try to think back and describe some circumstances. It might not have happened all at one time:

_____

MC   *3*

1   *4*

2   *5*

Impoverished environment

Enriched environment

Selection effect

Peer influence: taste/styles

Peer influence: accents/slang

Peer influence: substance use

Adolescence

Puberty

Moral reasoning

Lawrence Kohlberg

Preconventional morality

Conventional morality

Postconventional morality

Moral intuition

Moral action

Jonathan Haidt

You just got learned.

Translate the impoverished vs. enriched environment the rats were exposed to in the picture into human terms. How might you, as a parent, enrich a child's environment like the rat cage on the right?

_____

To what degree do you consider your environment growing up an impoverished or enriched one?

_____

The top comic on 510 seems like a funny joke and is, but couldn't you blame *all* the bad stuff you do on your environment growing up, if only you could prove- like the Behaviorists tried to do- that all of our behaviors are simple responses to external stimuli? How would you argue that in court? *Judge, I am innocent because...*

_____

If the judge were Martin Seligman from the quote on 510, do you think you'd be let off? _____

Pg. 513. You don't know when you transitioned from infancy to toddlerhood, necessarily, but you kinda know when you hit puberty. Describe when for females and males respectively.

_____

When you hit 30, which do you think you'll agree with more amongst G. Stanley Hall's choices?

_____ Why? _____
It starts with puberty, a physical alteration in a person's being, but when does it end?

_____

Why are people more prone to risk-taking in their teen years? Could you legit perp to your parents what the people in the comic on 514 are saying, that you're frontal lobes are *not fully matured*?

_____

If 'Junior' drives recklessly and academically self-destructs, Myers asks, and his parents freak out, do they have any reason to hope he might change in the next few years?

_____ why? _____ _____ _____

Alternatively, if Junior starts _____ heavily in his teen years, he's likely to go down the path of addiction and impulsivity well into his adult years because his frontal lobes will never develop to their potential. So don't start down that path. Seriously. Nike was wrong. Just Wait.

MC

1   3

2   4

Psychosocial stages _____

Trust _____

Autonomy _____

Initiative _____

Competence _____

Identity _____

Social identity _____

Different 'selves' _____

Intimacy _____

Emerging adulthood _____

Rite of passage _____

You just growed up.

Go back to 516 first of all. Review the Kohlberg stages here:

KOHLBERG STAGE   **DESCRIPTION**

1

2

3

519. Okay back to business. What did Erikson call the task of the adolescent? _____

American culture tends to be: *individualist*   *collectivist*   ...so we try on different _____

What does Myers mean when he says "I became conscious of my nationality when I was in Britain"

_____

Why was Myers conscious of his race when he was in Africa?

_____

520. What are Erikson's psychosocial tasks that must be fulfilled if one is to develop *normally*?

_____

What about Erikson's biography triggered his investigation into the search for identity?

_____

What is social identity?

_____

Look at the funkyzeit hairstyle on 521. Have you ever "tried on a self" like they have? How so?

_____

How did Erikson define 'intimacy?' _____

How is the comic on 523 saying the same (or a similar) thing as the graph on the same page?

_____

_____
                                    MC
1   *2*

3   *4*

5   *6*

X-chromosome _____

Y-chromosome _____

Testosterone _____

Primary sex characteristics _____

Secondary sex characteristics _____

Menarche _____

Spermarche _____

STDs _____

Factors predicting sexual restraint (4) _____

Hypersexualization _____

Sexual orientation _____

Environment and orientation _____

Biology and orientation _____

Depending on who you are, you're either going to want to skip this or you're going to be into it way to much. You know who you are.

Is menarche often a flashbulb memory in the history of a young woman? _____

The male equivalent is _____, which may also come as a surprise.
What does the growth of myelin at puberty mean for us?

_____

There are rare intersex individuals, give an example of how being one affected a person:

_____

What percentage of girls who were sexually experienced in their teenage years contracted an

SDC, according to the CDC: _____. The most common ones contracted are:

_____

While teen pregnancy was normal in caveman times, with the rise of civilization the age for having
children moved up. In Victorian times it moved up farther, to the point where now in the Western
world people view teen pregnancy as something almost scandalous. Is it fair to judge it like that?

_____

What are some contributing factors to teen pregnancy?

_____

Predictors of sexual restraint are: _____

Close up 531: It can be argued that modern society has exploited teen and even pre-teen girls in a
notoriously nasty way- by making their hypersexualization seem normal and perfectly fine. The
indicator a girl has been 'sexualized' by society is when she begins to:

1

2

3

_____

Contrast the environmental influence on sexual orientation vs. the biological influence:

_____

Compared with heterosexual people, homosexuals have been found to have these differences
(Table 53.1):

_____

Menopause _____

Aging and memory _____

Cross-sectional studies _____

Longitudinal studies _____

Terminal decline _____

Midlife transition _____

Social clock _____

Generativity _____

Integrity _____

At what age do people tend to 'peak' in their best physical condition _____

Describe some physical changes after age 40 when a person reaches middle adulthood:

_____

What physical changes happen in older adulthood?

_____

If you owned a store in the mall and didn't want teenage hoodlums and thugs hanging around it, driving away customers that actually buy something, what might you play over the speakers to discourage them from hanging around (besides classical music):

_____

Pg. 541 what are the two least safe decades for driving a car? _____and _____

Give an example of the ticking of the social clock:

On 544's comic, how would you feel at age 45 on your birthday, if you saw that ad? _____

What are some of the factors that increase the incidence of divorce in modern society?

_____

Do people who cohabitate (move in together) before they get married have a higher or lower rate

of divorce than those who wait until marriage? _____.

Red alert! Beep! Beep! Copy the biopsychosocial chart on 470 on how to "age successfully"

	MC	
1	*4*	
2	*5*	
3	*6*	*7*

Sigmund Freud _____

Psychoanalysis _____

Free association _____

Conscious mind _____

Unconscious mind _____

Preconscious _____

Id _____

Ego _____

Superego _____

Pleasure vs. Reality principle _____

Psychosexual stages (5) _____

Oedipus and Electra complex _____

Identification _____

Fixation _____

Defense mechanisms _____

Repression _____

Regression _____

Reaction formation _____

Projection _____

Rationalization _____

Displacement _____

Sublimation _____

Denial _____

Everybody's got one of them, or so we was meant to believe

What is Gamgee's personality like? _____

What is a personality anyway? _____

What are some terms in popular culture that we get directly from Freud and his personality
theory?

_____

How does Free Association work? (too bad tests in school aren't just 'free association'! right?

_____

How does the unconscious differ from the preconscious?

_____

Whereas you might call the id the "little devil", the superego the "little angel", and the ego the
'decider', how else does the iceberg pic describe these parts of the personality?

Id: *superego:*   *ego:*

The comic on 558 contains a "freudian slip". What was it? _____
By what principles did Freud argue the Id, Ego and Superego operate?

Id _____ *ego* _____ *superego* _____

The storyline in a dream is the manifest content, while _____
is the latent content, in Freud's dream theory.

The little devil in the other comic is working on the _____ principle to influence the dude.

A cat can be described as a hedonistic materialist. Which part of the three personality components

does a cat (and indeed most mammals) have the most of? _____. The least? _____

Whereas you might see a little kindergartener having fun pushing a lawnmower, Freud saw a

boy in the _____ stage, concerned with the _____ as his pleasure zone,

trying to cope with _____feelings for his mom, called the _____

complex, and secretly hating his dad (with the symbolic BIG mower), but at the same time starting

a process of _____ with dad and his patriarchal values. Yikes.

The Nazis collected and burned Freud's books in Germany in the 1930s, labeling them 'Jewish perversion.'
When Austria, where Freud lived, voted to join the Third Reich in the *Anschluss* of 1938, Freud left for
Britain on the Orient Express. Which of his theories are not widely accepted today either? (pg. 561):

Psychodynamic theories _____

Alfred Adler _____

Karen Horney _____

Neo-Freudians _____

Inferiority complex _____

Carl Jung _____

Collective unconscious _____

Human archetypes _____

Projective tests _____

Thematic Apperception Test _____

Rorschach Inkblot Test _____

False consciousness effect _____

Terror-management theory _____

You approach a romantic interest in college. You say, "let's have me talk about my personality. Module 56." She's like, "Oooh, I remember that one..."

The three big neo-Freudians are _____

Summarize the first: _____

Summarize the second: _____

Summarize the third: _____

What basic things did they reject from Freud's original psychoanalytic theory?

_____

What is a human archetype? _____
(btw Carl Jung had some really cool ideas if you look them up- Google Human Archetypes, or 12 common archetypes etc., which are you?)

A example of what a projective test measures: _____

Draw the Rorschach inkblot (meant to be disturbing by the way) on 567:
(Btw if you watch Crash Course Psychology, now you know what those things are Hank Green has hanging on the wall in his "office!")

1) What do you see? _____. 2) What might that reveal about you?

_____

What are some negative review given to the test by people in the field? Why did they say that?

_____

Is the test more than just a 'what is this inkblot' test? How?

_____

Summarize what is currently believed about the unconscious mind:

_____

_____

What is the function of a terror-management defense:

Humanistic theories

'Third Force'

Peak experiences

Client-centered perspective

Unconditional positive regard

Genuineness/acceptance/empathy

Ideal vs. actual self

Carl Rogers

There are some. And you should know them. For the test. On Friday. And yes it will help you marry 'up.'

The humanistic psychologists focused on _____ while Freud looked for 'sick' stuff.

What to healthy people strive for to the humanists? _____

What certain characteristics to Maslow's self-actualized people possess?

_____

Which psychologists emphasized human potential: 1)   2)

How did Carl Rogers say we could be 'genuine'? _____

Define unconditional positive regard: _____

Why is the dad in the comic on 572 not a good example of UPR?

_____

The humanistic perspective seems optimistic and nice. Why would there be criticism? What form do they take?

_____

In the comic taking place in what is apparently supposed to be representation of Hell, is the Devil

1) rationalizing, 2) legitimately surprised or 3) making a joke to Little Nicky? _____.

Do you agree with 1) the Christian philosophers who said people were prone to bad behavior (sin) by our nature and needed to be taught good morals so they can become better people, or 2) with philosopher Thomas Hobbes who said people are basically bad and need to be controlled by an imposing force to keep them in line through fear, or do you agree with 3) Jean Jacques Rousseau who argued people are basically good and virtuous and if they do bad things, it isn't because they were 'born bad,' but because their environment 'made them bad'? I agree with   *1   2   3*

If you believe 3 is correct, would you understand and sympathize if a judge let off a person convicted of stealing your car because their lawyer argued "my client's environment made him bad so he's not responsible for his own actions?"   *Y   N*

MC

1

2

3

4

Traits

Gordon Allport

Factor analysis

Unstable-stable

Extravert-introvert

Eysenck Personality Questionnaire

Heritability of personality

Personality inventory

MMPI

Empirically derived test

Costa and McCrae

Conscientiousness

Agreeableness

Neuroticism

Openness

Extraversion

Person-situation controversy

Music and personality

Bedroom/office and personality

Personal websites/personality

E-communication/personality

When Gordon Allport interviewed Freud so long ago, what troubled him about Freud's probing?

_____

Why did Gordon Allport not like Freud's theory of personality?

_____

What are *traits* (in general) in the trait perspective? _____

Stephen Colbert and Katy Perry are called extroverts. Think of a famous person who is an

introvert? _____. How about another one? _____.

What are the two spectrums on the Eysenck factor-analysis pie? _____

Where would you put yourself on the Eysenck factor analysis pie? (pick 2) _____ and

_____. Which two would you pick for Katy? _____ _____

Which traits would you select for a blind date?   ----------------------------   ----------------------------

Big 5: O   C   E   A   N
(581)
Look at the dimensions; pick one from each that represents you *more* than the others:

_____

The following basic research questions have been devised for application to the Big 5 trait theory:
     Question   *Answer*

1

2

3

What does Samuel Gosling think the following help us understand?

music preferences ---

bedrooms and offices---

websites / facebook---

email --
To what extent do you agree with this, on a 1-10 scale? _____. Look at the room on 584-
can you *judge* him? Can you *judge* your 'friend' by their *Facebook* page? You be the judge.

Social-cognitive perspective
_____

Behavioral approach
_____

Reciprocal determinism
_____

Albert Bandura
_____

Attributional style
_____

Excessive optimism
_____

Positive psychology
_____

Martin Seligman
_____

Self
_____

Spotlight effect
_____

Self-esteem
_____

Self-efficacy
_____

Self-serving bias
_____

Narcissism
_____

Defensive vs. secure self-esteem
_____

Individualism vs. collectivism
_____

Self (&I/C)
_____

Life task (&I/C)
_____

What matters (&I/C)
_____

Coping (&I/C)
_____

Morality (&I/C)
_____

Relationships (&I/C)
_____

Attributing behavior (&I/C)
_____

My environment gave me a good personality? Then you must've grown up in a slime pit!

Sum up the social-cognitive perspective:

_____

How do reciprocal influences work to mold our personalities in social-cognitive theory, and what is this called?

_____

You do have some control in this process. Summarize Out the three ways individuals and the environment interact, and state which portion of the interaction do you control most:

1

2

3

_____

How much control will you have over your life in 3 years compared to now: _____

List cases of excessive optimism: _____

What does the comic on 589 encourage us to do? _____

Is Seligman onto something with positive psychology, or is he a quack? Opinion:

_____

Most homicidal maniacs are, according to the FYI,   *a. prone to anger*   *b. just snapped*

The AP Exam Tip says study the big charts on 593. Ready? Go. How long did you stare _____

Is the girl wearing the Barry Manilow shirt on 594:   *a. a hipster*   *b. a fan*

Did it turn out that people noticed and ridiculed the girl for wearing the uncool shirt?   *a. yes b. no*

So basically she fell victim to the _____ Effect, and should lose some _____ Esteem.

In the comic on 597, which ones of the 8 have YOU said? Be honest now! ☺

Intelligence
_____

Intelligence test
_____

General intelligence (*g*)
_____

Factor analysis
_____

Charles Spearman
_____

L.L. Thurstone
_____

Satoshi Kanazawa
_____

Savant syndrome
_____

Howard Gardner
_____

Multiple Intelligences (8)
_____

Existentialist (a new one)
_____

Grit
_____

Robert Sternberg
_____

Triarchic theory
_____

Analytical intelligence
_____

Creative intelligence
_____

Practical intelligence
_____

Emotional intelligence
_____

Brain size and intelligence
_____

Neural processing speed and intelligence
_____

Do you have enough to get started right away? Or do you need some negative reinforcement?

What do *you* think intelligence is? _____

What is *'g'* intelligence? _____
How did factor analysis help Spearman in his quest to understand what intelligence is?

_____

What did Thurstone do to try and disprove Spearman's *g* intelligence?

_____

What was the 'persistent tendency' that kept reappearing in Thurstone's work that actually confirmed the existence of *'g'*?

_____

What did Robert Plomin say about *'g'* in 1999:	How 'bout Satoshi Kanazawa say about *'g'* in 2010:
	DANG *'g'*!

Another theory of intelligence was done by Gardner. His theory is called _____

Check out the chart on 526. Rate yourself on the 9 intelligences, from 1 to 9, with 9 being your strongest and 1 being your weakest- use each number only one time:

linguistic	*musical*	*logical/math*	*visual/spatial*	*movement*

Interpersonal	*intrapersonal*	*naturalist*	*existentialist**

* a 9th was recently added.

In Sternberg's Triarchic Theory, what are the 3 types? _____

How did Sternberg describe analytical intelligence? _____

What about creative intelligence? _____

What about practical intelligence? _____
Scan over the green-blue table on pg. 614. Out of the four theories of intelligence, which ones do you think is most accurate as to the real situation?

1)   2)   3)   4)

Define emotional intelligence _____

There are four components to Emo intelligence. Note them in the space below:

Natural ability _____

Francis Galton _____

Alfred Binet _____

Mental age _____

Lewis Terman _____

I.Q. _____

Stanford-Binet test _____

Eugenics _____

WWI/Immigrant I.Q. tests _____

Achievement test _____

Aptitude test _____

Wechsler Adult Intelligence Test _____

Standardization _____

Normal (bell) curve _____

Flynn effect _____

Reliability _____

Validity _____

Content validity _____

Predictive validity _____

Criterion _____

SAT test _____

GRE test _____

The picture on 617- is that a familiar sight? He ha ho... its all a conspiracy to keep you do... cile

Do you agree with Plato's quote? _____.

Francis Galton wanted high ability, intelligent people to mate with one another to preserve human intelligence. He believed intelligence was mostly   *inherited*   *environmental*

What was the thesis of Galton's book? _____

How did Alfred Binet revolutionize our understanding of intelligence? _____

What was Lewis Terman's contribution? _____

Write the Stanford-Binet method of calculating IQ (618):   = _____ x

What is the major problem with this method? _____

What does the Wechsler test do to measure IQ? _____

What is an aptitude test vs. an achievement test? _____

What looks like the hardest part of the Wechsler test on pg. 620? _____

On the bell curve (also called the _____ curve, and in math the Gaussian curve), if a

person scored an 85 on the Wechsler test, they would be: _____ standard deviation(s) from the norm.

What are some speculations as to why the Flynn Effect was observed in the 20th century?

_____

Now read all of figure 61.3. See how they tossed in that last bit? Hmm...

What do Lynn and Harvey (2008) predict about the future of IQ scores from a genetic-heredity perspective?

_____

Summarize the reliability of these standardized intelligence tests, citing evidence from 622:

_____

Likewise, summarize the validity of standardized intelligence tests, citing evidence:

_____

MODULE 62   **DYNAMICS OF INTELLIGENCE: Pg. 625**   NAME_____

Cohort
_____

Fluid intelligence
_____

Crystalized intelligence
_____

Intellectual disability
_____

Down syndrome
_____

Dependent personality
_____

Gifted
_____

MODULE 63   **GENETIC AND ENVIRONMENTAL INFLUENCES: Pg. 632**   NAME_____

Heritability of intelligence
_____

Genius
_____

Polygenetic trait
_____

Environmental influences
_____

Epigenetics
_____

Twin studies and intelligence
_____

Carol Dwick
_____

MODULE 64   **GROUP DIFFERENCES: Pg. 638**   NAME_____

Gender differences
_____

Racial differences
_____

Bias controversy
_____

Stereotype threat
_____

Culture-neutral questions
_____

Race: social or biological construct?
_____

Are you going to be a smart alec about this? Good! It's actually okay this time.

Describe why Wechsler's cross-sectional study confounded our understanding of intellectual stability for many decades:

_____

Conversely, describe the findings of longitudinal studies:

_____

Give some examples of fluid intelligence:

Give some examples of crystalized intelligence:

_____

"With age, we lose and we win." How so?

_____

Dynamics of intelligence: what is a better predictor of early reading ability (circle one):
　　　　A. being able to talk early　　　　*B. having parents who read to the child a lot*

What happens around age 4? _____

On 627 and in the FYI box, note the stability of SAT tests taken at age 17-18 and the GRE (Graduate Readiness Exam) taken at age 23-24, which are known to predict each other better than they predict school achievement. This means they are (circle): 　　*reliable*　　　*valid*

What amazing thing happened in Scotland regarding the stability of IQ over the life span:

_____

Do Scottish women with higher IQ scores live longer or shorter average lives? _____

Are test scores at age 11 a good predictor of whether you will live past 70?　　*Yes*　　　*No*

What is mental retardation now called? _____. What is its incidence? _____

What is the cause of Down syndrome? _____

Would a eugenicist like Galton have argued Down syndrome patients should have children? _____

What is mainstreaming? _____

When Terman studied 1500 high-IQ California kids, what did he find?

Be careful. If its genetics, pick a good mate. If its environment, pick a good mate.

Is the comic on 632 funny? Rate it 1 (not funny) -5 (very funny): _____

Intelligence tends to run in families: *True*   *False*

According to the twin studies, how much of intelligence is inherited: _____

Are A. twins raised apart closer in intelligence or B. non-related siblings raised in the same environment?   *A.*   *B.*

How might a person arguing for environment use twin studies to bolster their case?

_____

_____

Intelligence is polygenetic, meaning _____

In the nature/nurture balance, which seems to win out the long term re: intelligence _____

Is the comic on 633 funny? Rate it 1 (not funny) -5 (very funny): _____

The genetic component (heritability) of intelligence grows to _____ percent by adulthood.

What was the goal of Hunt's *tutored human enrichment* program? _____

In which countries have orphanages increased the attractiveness of potential adoptees by using tutored human enrichment?

_____

What was the goal of *Baby Einstein* vs. *Head Start?* Was either successful?

_____

The *Mozart Effect* (i.e.: playing Mozart and other classical music to babies and kids gets their synapses connecting) has been shown to work. Then it was shown by another study not to matter. Later it was shown to work again. Is there a lesson here?

_____

MC

1   *3*

2   *4*

*People brag when they do better than other **individuals**, but bragging when your **race** does better than others? What is this, the **Olympics**?*

Are there group differences that Myers and other psychologists feel can't be ignored?   Y   N

In the male-female gap: who tests higher in the following:

Spelling   *Verbal ability*   *Nonverbal ability*

Sensation   *Emotion-detection*   *Math and spatial*

Extreme high intelligence   *Computation*   *Extreme low intelligence*

How does evolutionary psychologist Geary explain male superiority in large-scale spatial relations?

_____

How does evolutionary psychologist Geary explain female domination in location and finding things?

_____

According to the picture on 639, most computer geeks are _____.
Why does this fact support the nature side of the argument over the nurture?

_____

Name the two disturbing facts fueling the group-differences by race and ethnicity:

1)   *2)*

What is the white group average? _____; For blacks: _____; For Hispanics? _____

Pg. 641. "Cultures rise and fall, genes do not". Do you agree? _____
                                        (if you do, don't look up *Degeneration Theory*, probably the scariest thing you never heard of)

Would Galton agree? _____
Which one of the three 'camps' do you most agree with on the topic of race and intelligence- That the differences in intelligence are 1) genetically transmitted, 2) socially influenced or that 3) the tests are biased in favor of one group or against another and therefore invalid?

                                                _____

Which of the two meanings of bias do you see as the better one (don't be biased now!):

_____

What does the latest research show concerning the scientific meaning of bias and the predictive *validity* of modern IQ tests?

_____

Would you feel more pressure (stereotype threat) if it seemed to you that you were representing not just yourself but also your 'race', 'ethnicity', 'gender' or other biological group by the outcome?

Psychological disorder

Maladaptive behavior

ADHD

Medical model

DSM-5

Diagnostic label

Insanity and responsibility

Immigrant paradox

Is this assignment, for example, abnormal?

Explain how the definition of *psychological disorder* tries to make sure that something 'wrong' with people due to a regular life situation- like sadness at the death of a relative- is *not* counted as a disorder:

_____

_____

In your opinion, how many times per regular school day can one use hand cleaner or go to the bathroom to wash their hands before something moves from 'germ-o-phobe- to disorder? _____

How many years ago was homosexuality taken off the APA list of psych disorders? _____

In the pics on 651, all four of the guys are bragging in their own way to women, showing themselves off. Why might women from their respective cultures be interested in them?

_____

652 ADHD box. Are you for or against drug administration? Summarize:
Evidence cited by pro-ADHD people   Evidence cited by anti-ADHD people

_____

What do you think about the ADHD controversy?

_____

What is psychopathology? _____

Some 'disorders' are culture-based. What is Taijin-kyofu-sho? _____
What is Susto? _____

What is Amok? _____

If a woman cuts herself because she thinks it helps her relieve anxious feelings, but knows it is not

a good idea to do so, this is _____ disorder.

Biopsychosocial box! Biopsychosocial Box! Sketch in the Biopsychosocial Box! on pg. 654:

_____

Today, psychologists diagnose disorders using the DSM, which stands for _____

The DSM really gets detailed on when something is and when something is not a psych disorder. If you walk into a clinic and tell them you "can't sleep," they are going to want to know if it is insomnia disorder or something else. What is the minimum number of questions they'll have to ask you just to see if clinical insomnia may be the issue? _____.

What is the danger of 'pathologizing' everyday life?

_____

Have you been labeled as anything? (You don't have to answer) but if you have or have not, or know someone who has, to what extent do you think people internalize the labels placed on them and make them part of their identity? Does it become a self-fulfilling prophecy, like stereotype threat in the intelligence chapter with the test taking?

_____

On 657 there is a list of disorder types and the percentage of people in the USA who say they have them. Rank them in order, with 'Any' at the top.

DISORDER   **PERCENTAGE**   **HAVE I HEARD OF IT? (Y OR N)**

Extra work (not credit, *work*- there's a difference.): the DSM V has 18 categories of disorders that it covers. Section 2 of 3 is the key section where they all are. Look up online the 18 and list them below:

Anxiety disorder _____

GAD _____

Panic disorder _____

Phobia _____

Agoraphobia _____

OCD _____

Obsessions _____

Compulsions _____

Perfectionism _____

PTSD _____

Trauma _____

Survivor resiliency _____

Post-traumatic growth _____

Social anxiety disorder _____

Getting nervous?

Give an example of what can happen when a person has the following disorder by describing a situation in which it might trigger anxiety in a person- "set the scene":

GAD   *Panic Disorder*

Arachnophobia   *Ophidiophobia*

Acrophobia: *Claustrophobia:*

Agoraphobia: *Social phobia:*

OCD: *PTSD:*

664. Give an example of an obsession: _____

Give an example of a compulsion: _____

The 3 major obsessions are: *The three major compulsions are:*

(Anyone OCD enough to notice and be annoyed by the use of '3' on the left and 'three' on the right?)

Mood disorder _____

Major depressive disorder _____

Dysthymia _____

Bipolar disorder _____

Mania _____

Disruptive mood dysregulation disorder _____

Prozac/Zoloft/Paxil _____

Self-defeating beliefs _____

Rumination _____

Overthinking _____

Explanatory style _____

Vicious cycle of depressed thinking _____

Kay Redfield Jamison _____

Now don't get no somatoform disorder just cause we're learnin' 'bout this bad mood stuff

Define major depressive disorder: _____

Give an example of MDD: _____

672. Darwin Quote: Why is depression like a shield for us?

Summarize the six symptoms depression, two of which must persist for a long time:

*   *

*   *

*   *

How is bi-polar disorder (manic depression) different? _____

What is mania? _____

Note some symptoms of the manic phase: _____

Do you think the spike in bi-polar diagnoses likely to end now that the DSM's new edition is out?

Is there a correlation between high creativity and bipolar disorder?   Y   N

People who rely on precision and logic, such as _____ are less bipolar

than people who rely on _____ and _____

like _____.

What evidence says depression has a biological cause? _____
(**nature**)

What evidence supports the social-cognitive perspective? _____
(**nurture**)
676 box. the most genetic of the mood disorders is _____

How does learned helplessness lead to self-defeating beliefs? _____

Link rumination to depression's vicious cycle: _____

Have you ever felt depressed?   To what extent does pg. 681 help explain why?

Schizophrenia
_____

Psychosis
_____

Delusions
_____

Paranoia
_____

Word salad
_____

Hallucinations
_____

Flat affect vs. Catatonia
_____

Chronic vs. acute schizophrenia
_____

Biological causes
_____

I'm hearing a voice. Its saying… "Gut… oh… orc…" in a Scottish accent

What symptoms characterize schizophrenia? _____

Give an example of the following:

Delusions   *Paranoia*

Word salad   *Hallucinations*

Is the puzzle-face on 685 really that disturbing? Why or why not?

_____

What are some inappropriate emotions or actions? _____

What's the difference between chronic and acute schizophrenia?

_____

The primary cause of schizophrenia is: _____

Summarize the issue with levels of dopamine in schizophrenic patients

_____

How is it genetic? _____

How is it psychological?_____

Psychologists have found seven (7) symptoms that have been judged as early warning signs of schizophrenia. List them, and indicate if you know anyone with the symptom:

1

2

3

4

5

6

7

Somatic symptom disorder _____

Conversion disorder _____

Illness anxiety disorder _____

Dissociative disorder _____

DID _____

Fugue state _____

Eating disorder _____

Anorexia _____

Bulimia nervosa _____

Binge-eating disorder _____

Personality disorder _____

Antisocial personality disorder _____

Avoidant personality disorder _____

Schizoid personality disorder _____

Narcissistic personality disorder _____

Histrionic personality disorder _____

Conscience _____

_____

_____

_____

_____

_____

"Well, I've got antisocial personality disorder, but most of the time it stays quiet." –Worst job interview answer... ever

When anxiety in your mind converts into a physical symptom, its called _____

Over the weekend, I interpreted my stomach growling as a dreaded disease. I may have _____

If someone calls me a hypochondriac because I am always on WebMD checking for all the things the twitch in my back muscle could be, or the swollen lymph node, then the official term for what that person should be calling me is:

_____ Are you one? _____

People with a dissociative disorder might be seen...

Give an example of a fugue state _____

Last test everyone was excited about the possible answer 'DID' because it was on the word wall. But we DIDn't go over that one yet! Now we are. Here it is. DID is:

_____ , in which a person...

What did DID used to be called? _____
Nick Spanos and other psychologists began doubting that DID was real. What evidence did they cite:

In a more normal way, do you ever 'flip' from displaying one personality to another? When?

_____
We have a phrase, taken from Shakespeare in the box. He said in Hamlet:

_____ We say: *"There is _____ to the _____ "*

If one has anorexia, they are likely to: _____

If they have bulimia nervosa, they are likely to: _____

What is binge-eating disorder _____

What demographic groups are most at risk for these? _____

Most women said they would rather have a 'perfect body' than for their mate to have one. Most men said the opposite. This reflect the selfishness of women and the overall giving nature of men, doesn't it?
_____why?_____

List the personality disorders: _____

If one has antisocial personality disorder, they are likely to: | Fig. 12.11. Why is this scary?
                                                                    |
                                                                    |

Psychotherapy _____

Biomedical therapy _____

Eclectic approach _____

Psychoanalytic therapy _____

Resistance _____

Interpretation _____

Transference _____

Psychodynamic therapy _____

Face-to-face therapy _____

Humanistic therapy _____

Insight therapies _____

Self-fulfillment _____

'Client' vs. 'Patient' _____

'Responsibility' vs. 'blame' _____

'Conscious' over 'unconscious' _____

'Present' vs. 'Past' _____

Client-centered therapy _____

Active listening _____

Unconditional positive regard _____

Paraphrase/clarify/reflect _____

Dorothea Dix _____

Carl Rogers _____

Mary Cover Jones _____

You're about to be treated. And you may not like it. And it might not help. "Ow."

How did Kay Redfield Jamison beat bi-polar disorder? _____

We've measured the size of the earth, charted the heavens, cracked the genetic code but we've treated psych disorders by...

Psychotherapy is _____, while

Biomedical therapy is _____.

_____% of psychologist take eclectic approach, which is _____

Think back to 1920. Those were the days- WWI just ended, and Freud invented psychoanalysis.

What were the aims of psychoanalysis? _____

Describe what Freud would do to people _____

	Phenomenon	*Example*
Resistance		
Interpretation		
Transference		

How long does psychoanalysis take to 'work'? _____. There are: lots / not many.
Luckily we have the psychodynamic neo-Freudians, who still operate. How are they:
SIMILAR   *DIFFERENT*

Humanistic psychotherapy is a little different too. They use insight therapies, which are:

Since they believe everyone has an unrealized potential and that it would make them happy if they could find it was and then pursue it, they focus on:

_____

Carl Rogers used the word _____, as opposed to "patients," because that term sounds less like the person is a schmuck who needs help and more of a business partner trying to achieve a goal.
Who would use CCA? _____

Read the Rogers-Client exchange. Is he being nice, mean or other? _____

List people with whom or situations in which *you* might use unconditional positive regard:

Behavior therapy
_____

Counterconditioning
_____

Exposure therapy
_____

Systematic desensitization
_____

Progressive relaxation
_____

Virtual reality exposure therapy
_____

Aversive conditioning
_____

Behavior modification
_____

Token economy
_____

Cognitive therapy
_____

Inoculation training
_____

Rational-emotive behavior therapy
_____

Self-defeat/catastrophizing
_____

Revealing/testing/changing beliefs
_____

Aaron Beck
_____

Joseph Wolpe
_____

Albert Ellis
_____

Group therapy
_____

'Social laboratory'
_____

Family therapy
_____

Self-help group
_____

Meta-analysis
_____

Therapeutic alliance

Aversive conditioning? Yeah- this is the good stuff

Time for some behavior modification: Pavlov- Awake! Thorndike- Awake! Skinner- Awake! We have someone here with a phobia of confined spaces, and they won't go into an elevator. What do we do?

        Skinner's ghost*: "Be calm, my child. We're about to scare that there fear right out of them!"*

Describe counterconditioning _____

        Example: _____

Describe exposure therapy _____

        Example: _____

Describe virtual reality exposure therapy _____

        Example: _____

Describe aversive conditioning _____

        Example: _____

Provide an example of how a token economy would help with behavior modification during operant conditioning:

_____

While behavior therapy focuses on the stimulus-response dynamic, cognitive therapy focuses on these things:

_____

Give an example of REBT_____

In cognitive therapy, they gonna get chya mind right. They gonna get Morgan Freeman up in there and he's gonna talk those catastrophizing thoughts outta there, so you can focus on the good stuff. Read the Beck-Client exchange. By what mechanism does it "cure" depression?

_____

_____

How is stress inoculation training a good example of a cognitive therapy?

_____

Which of the techniques in the table on 722 do you think would be most effective on *you*? _____

Some advantages of group therapy: Some successful self-help groups:

Even if you evaluate it poorly, you still have to pay. That's the good part.

What are three reasons that we might tend to believe psychotherapies are more effective than they really are?

1   *2*   *3*

What was the surprising finding of the Joan McCord research on whether counseling helped boys who committed juvenile crime:

_____

Did Eysenck's study help confirm this research or did it go against it? _____

Give an example of a meta-analysis: _____

In the box on 730, Kahneman said this about regression toward the mean:

_____

Is the dodo bird from Alice in Wonderland right? _____

Which 'therapies' have no scientific support: _____

Define evidence-based practice: _____

Is practicing EMDR evidence-based? _____. Is using light therapy evidence-based? _____
(Anyone would 'like' to be prescribed a 'vacation'; so maybe we can start a SAD Psychology clinic?)

All psychotherapists aim to provide these three essential things:

1   *2*   *3*

_____

How can culture influence the therapist-client relationship?

_____

How can gender influence the therapist-client relationship?

_____

Extra Effort: Go to PsychologyToday.com and click 'find a therapist' in your area. Name the person you'd go to if you wanted to sign up for counseling.

_____ What made you pick that one? _____

Psychopharmacology _____

Antipsychotic drug _____

Dardive dyskinesia _____

Antianxiety drug _____

Xanax/Ativan _____

Antidepressant _____

Prozac/Zoloft/Paxil _____

SSRIs _____

Mood-stabilizer _____

Lithium/Depakote _____

Electroconvulsive therapy _____

Repetitive transcranial magnetic stimulation _____

Psychosurgery _____

Lobotomy _____

Therapeutic lifestyle change _____

*Aerobic exercise _____

*Sleep _____

*Light exposure _____

*Social connection _____

*Anti-rumination _____

*Nutrition _____

73 - BIOMEDICAL THERAPIES NAME_____

When all else fails, use drugs*

The term for the study of how drugs affect people's minds and behavior is _____

Why are the people in the comic on 740 so happy? Are they really "happy"? What else might they "be?"

_____

When does a person have a psychosis: _____

What does Thorazine do biologically? _____

What do antipsychotics mimic well enough to fool the receptor? _____

What is tardive dyskinesia? _____

What other neurotransmitter do the new atypical antipsychotics target? _____

What are some side effects of these drugs? _____

Name some common anti-anxiety drugs: _____

Name some common anti-depressant drugs: _____

Aside from anti-depressant drugs, how else can a person 'give themselves a lift?'

_____

Chart on 742: draw the shape of serotonin _____ Draw the shape of Prozac: _____
How is it that Prozac affects serotonin levels if they are different shapes?

_____

Rate the comic on 743:   *Funny*   *Not funny*   *I love this class and all its content*

The amazingly sad statistic is that around 30,000 people take their
own lives yearly in America. For bi-polar patients the rate is far higher.
What is the suicide rate of bi-polar patients not taking lithium vs. taking it? _____ vs _____

What is ECT? _____. When was it first used? _____. How many volts? _____

Describe the procedure for rTMS: _____

Give an example of a psychosurgery:_____

What happens in a lobotomy? _____

How do you feel? _____
prescribed by a certified psychiatrist for a legitimate reason

Social psychology

_____

Attribution theory

_____

Fundamental attribution error

_____

Attitudes

_____

Central route persuasion

_____

Peripheral route persuasion

_____

'Attitudes follow behavior'

_____

Foot-in-the door

_____

Door-in-the-face

_____

Role

_____

Zimbardo Prison Experiment

_____

Cognitive dissonance

_____

Leon Festinger

_____

You got a bad attitude? Then I'm about to make the fundamental attribution error. And you ain't gonna like it.

Dirk Willems' story is that he _____
    Are our lives "connected by a thousand invisible threads?" Did the Willems story affect you at all? Think about it.

That's well interesting. What is attribution theory?

_____

If a teacher metaphorically smacks down a young buck who is overexcited due to a combination of hormones, metabolically processed sugars and an overall boredom with public K-12 education, the teacher might *attribute* the bad behavior to a dispositional- or situational- source. What are examples of these?

Dispositional: _____   *Situational:* _____

Describe the fundamental attribution error we humanoids tend to make:

_____

Give examples of FAE from the text and the comic on 755:

_____

After behaving badly ourselves, we tend to attribute our behavior to _____

Political conservatives are likely to say _____ cause crime and should be accountable.

Political liberals are more likely to say _____ influence people to perform the criminal acts. Does this remind you in any way of nature-nurture?   Y   N

Do you have any distinctive attitudes? _____

How are people convinced of something? Look at the defs of CRP and PRP and then think of a commercial or ad that used each. Describe it briefly:

    CRP: _____

    PRP: _____

Actions affect attitudes dude. Do attitudes follow behavior?   Y   N

Give an example of the foot in the door phenomenon: Now draw a foot in a door:

_____
What 'roles' have you played out recently? _____

At first, a new role may feel _____ to us, but as we play it out, we embody it more and more.
What did Zimbardo's Prison experiment reveal?

_____

Why is the Iraq War (2005-2012) used as an example of cognitive dissonance?

Conformity

Nonconformity

Asch Conformity experiment

Normative social influence

Informational social influence

Obedience

Milgram Obedience experiment

Birkenhead drill

Solomon Asch: **Stanley Milgram:**   **Philip Zimbardo:**

"Conform. Obey." –Whatever you do, do NOT Youtube the following: They Live Sunglasses.
And if you do… don't tell **anyone** how you found out

Usually people don't like being labeled 'conformists', but is all conformity bad? How do you conform at school in a way that is beneficial to you and the community?

Describe the chameleon effect: _____

According to the comic, is getting a tattoo or piercing a rebellious act, or a sign of individual expression, or is it conformity? Why?

Group pressure and conformity. Describe the findings of Ashe's conformity experiment (the dude in the middle is like "*whaaaaaat...*"):

What 7 conditions tend to strengthen conformity?

A example of normative social influence is:	An example of informational social influence is:

Describe the findings of Milgram's Obedience Experiment:

Are the Milgram findings scary to you at all?   *Y*   *N*

Milgram concluded obedience was highest when four qualifications are met, namely:

1

2

3

4

Social facilitation _____

Social loafing _____

Deindividuation _____

Group polarization _____

Groupthink _____

Power of Situation vs. Individual _____

Culture _____

Preservation of innovation _____

Norms _____

Culture shock _____

Identify some examples of group behavior in your own life. Are you a fan of anything?

List a good example of social facilitation:

When have you been enhanced by social facilitation? _____

Should we be surprised by the chart on 772? Why or why not?

List a good example of social loafing:

When have you socially loafed? _____

The three reasons identified for social loafing are: 1)

2)   3)

Don't you love when you have group work in a class and one kid doesn't do anything?   *Y   N*

How are social facilitation and social loafing kind of like opposites?

Note times when, in general, deindividuation is more likely to occur:

You know how if you are hanging out with people who like Star Trek, and they are threatening the people who like Star Wars with a Vulcan nerve pinch, while the Star Wars people are threatening the Star Trek people with a Jedi mind trick, both groups get all riled up about how great their side is? In fact, later that day when their family asked them how much they liked their show, they'd tend to say they liked it MORE than the previous day, before the incident happened. This is called

_____ _____. Have you been polarized like that? _____

Any kids in class very polarized on a political issue? What is it? _____

Is it surprising that after a political rally like the DNC or RNC,
supporters feel even more strongly loyal to their particular side? _____. Didn't think so.
What about the Challenger explosion does Myers attribute to groupthink?

Has groupthink ever made you feel like a group you were a part of- or observed- made the wrong (i.e.: stupid) decision because some people dominated the group that really didn't have any freaking idea what they were talking about?

Describe a time: Name some of your norms:

Prejudice _____

Discrimination _____

Stereotype _____

Ethnocentrism _____

Sex-selective abortions _____

Just-world phenomenon _____

Ingroup vs. outgroup _____

Ingroup bias _____

Scapegoat theory _____

Blame-the-victim dynamic _____

Other-race effect _____

The Beatles: "All you need is love; all you need is love; all you need is love, love, love is all you need"
Rammstein: "Mein land! Mein land! Du bist hier in meinem land!" (Do not Youtube this in class).

Give an example of prejudice _____Give an example of a stereotype_____

Give an example of discrimination _____

Which race was least likely to marry someone out of their own group in 2010? _____
Summarize how public attitudes in America have changed regarding racially mixed dating since 1987:

_____

So that's it right? Almost no one is prejudiced anymore! Yippee! Oh wait, what's the difference
between overt and implicit prejudice?

_____

Would you (or your relatives) be okay with marrying someone outside your race (old term:
miscegenation, new term: exogamy)? Or would there be some consternation? Why?

_____

After 9/11 what traits did many Americans ascribe to Muslims? _____

What traits did many Muslims ascribe to Americans and Europeans? _____

What kind of discrimination do women face in Saudi Arabia? _____
Close Up 782. How did the white college girls patronize the black essay writer? Is that prejudice?

_____

What accounts for the missing women phenomenon in Asia since 1980? Does it involve prejudice?

_____

What is the social position of someone most likely to promote the just-world phenomenon?

_____

Do you have any ingroups? _____; How 'bout outgroups _____

What might your ingroup bias be? _____

Name some cliques formed by high schoolers: _____

What do chimpanzees do when they are touched by a member of an outgroup? _____

Give an example of scapegoat theory in action: _____

At what age does does the other race effect start? _____

In some Islamic countries, women who are raped can be charged with _____ and executed. ☹

         NAME_____

Aggression
_____

Genetic influences
_____

Neural influences
_____

Biochemical influences
_____

Aversive events
_____

Frustration-aggression principle
_____

Social scripts
_____

What are the arguments surrounding the following examples:

X-Rated materials: *Video games:*

*Alright everyone let's get started. **I SAID GET STARTED!!!***

Give examples of aggression: _____

What aside from physical violence is it? _____

What is the single most common genetic marker for aggression in humans? _____

Do you agree with the comic on 790, or does it overstate? _____

What is funny about the monkey experiment in 'neural influences' section?

_____

What is the relationship between frontal lobes of the brain and aggression?

_____

What happens to the aggression levels in male animals (and male humans- ever heard of a eunuch?) when they are castrated?

_____

What kind of face type is most linked to aggression? _____

The biochemical hormone linked to increased aggression is _____.

If someone gets bumped while shuffling past people in a crowd, they are more likely to respond negatively if they:

    Have been drinking alcohol   *Have not been drinking*

How long did it take for the black penguins to stop discriminating against the white one? _____

Give some examples of the frustration-aggression principle.

 From the book: *From the story of your life:*

_____

How would your parent(s) respond to the 'parent training program' situation on pg. 792?

_____

Are social scripts different for men and women? Give some examples:

_____

How does the pornography industry, now valued at _____ billion dollars, act as a 'media model?'

_____

Look up the case of the guy who trained to kill people by playing video games on 794, Anders Breivik. What was his motivation?

Mere exposure effect _____

Proximity _____

Physical attractiveness _____

Similarity _____

Passionate vs. companionate love _____

Equity _____

Self-disclosure _____

Eros _____

Ludus _____

Pragma _____

Storge _____

Agape _____

Mania _____

79 – ATTRACTION NAME_____

"You're lips are venomous poison" –Alice Cooper

What are the big three factors that influence attraction?

1   *2*   *3*

_____

The idea that familiarity breeds fondness is called, in psychological language, the _____

Why did the chair on pg. 800 become a bestseller? _____

What does it mean that 'income analyses show a penalty for plainness or obesity and a premium on beauty?'

_____

Which do Americans spend more on: *education*   *beauty supplies*

What do men tend to look for in women vs. what women tend to look for in men?

_____

Attraction- Circle one: *Opposites Attract*   *Birds of a Feather Flock Together*

What's the difference between passionate and companionate love?

_____

Figure it out: *A. Commitment*   *B. Intimacy*   *C. Passion*

____ feelings that promote closeness and connection, confiding in others and sharing feelings

____ the intense desire for union with another person, erotic attraction

____ decision to maintain a relationship over a long term, intention to remain together

Figure it out: A. *Eros*   B. *Ludus*   C. *Storge*   D. *Agape*   E. *Pragma*   F. *Mania*

___ playful love   ___ passion and desire love   ___ practical love

___ companionship love   ___ altruistic, selfless love   ___ demanding, possessive love

_____

How would a person know 'equity' if they saw it:

How would someone know 'self-disclosure' if they saw it:

Altruism

Bystander effect

Diffusion of responsibility

Assumption of responsibility

Social exchange theory

Reciprocity norm

Social-responsibility norm

Conflict

Social trap

Mirror-image perceptions

Self-fulfilling prophecy

Contact theory

Superordinate goal

GRIT

If you are ultra altruistic, that is something to brag about... constantly

How does Carl Wilkens's story illustrate altruism? _____

_____

How does Paul Ruseabagina's story illustrate altruism? _____

Have you ever been altruistic? When? _____

The opposite is not helping, known as the _____ effect.

Which students were most likely to help in the staged epileptic seizure experiment?

_____

Think of a time you witnessed 'diffusion of responsibility': _____
When are we most likely to help?   (opposite situation) when are we least likely to help?

1

2

3

4

5

6

7

8

Provide an example of reciprocity norm: And now one for social-responsibility norm:

_____   _____

How much does the world spend per day in lessening or causing conflict? _____
Look at the non-zero sum game on 811.
If you had the choice of A or B, where in A you get
5bucks and in B you get 10, which would you pick? _____

An example of a mirror-image perception: _____

An example of a self-fulfilling prophecy: _____

An example of a superordinate goal: _____

MODULE 81   **INFLUENCES OF DRUG USE: Pg. 822**   NAME_____

Biological influences _____

Psychological influences _____

Social-cultural influences _____

MODULE 82   **PSYCHOLOGY AT WORK: Pg. 827**   NAME_____

Work as a job _____

Work as a career _____

Work as a calling _____

Flow _____

Mihaly Csikszentmihalyi _____

I/O psychology _____

Personnel focus _____

Organizational focus _____

Human Factors focus _____

Strength discovery _____

Structured interviews _____

Performance appraisal _____

Achievement motivation _____

Grit _____

Engaged employee _____

Not engaged _____

Actively disengaged _____

Task vs. Social leadership _____

Two dimensions of arousal _____

Catharsis _____

Feel-good/do-good phenomenon _____

Subjective well-being _____

Materialism _____

Diminishing returns phenomenon _____

Adaptation-level phenomenon _____

Relative deprivation _____

Happiness tendencies _____

Financial realization _____

Time control _____

Acting happy _____

Engagement _____

Aerobic exercise _____

Enhanced sleep _____

Cultivate relationships _____

Focus beyond self _____

Blessings catalog _____

Spirituality _____

David Myers _____

_____

_____

_____

Health psychology _____

Pessimism _____

Optimism _____

Role of social support _____

Laughter therapy _____

Pet therapy _____

Relaxation therapy _____

Aerobic exercise therapy _____

Meditation _____

Faith factor _____

Alternative medicine _____

Tool-using animals _____

Ape vocabularies _____

Chimp signing _____

Comprehending canine _____

*Remember: It is not enough to look up these online! Tests are based off the book and the AP World curriculum, so while checking online is fine, it is imperative your understanding of the significant of these vocab terms and concepts reflects the context of how each applies to the chapter specifically...

Part II

Addenda: Extra Resources

Crash Course Guide

Reviewer _____

It's Review Time!

Topic of today's episode _____

Preview: From my memory logs about what we have been talking about this week, I predict Hank Green will be talking about topics like:

_____

Some things he covered that were not in the book or talked about in class were these:

_____

What silly (or not so silly) gimmicks did Mr. Green have this time?

_____

How did those items or gimmicks tie-in to the material in the chapter?

_____

_____

_____

After Watching:

  a)   Was there a 'deep' lesson at the very end? What was it?

  b)   To me, the most interesting part of this chapter, the thing most

        relevant to my life, is _____ because:

Test Correction Guide

Corrector_____

Time to get it right!

Test Name_____

Directions: Identify the numbers of the answers you got wrong on the test and write them:

Number   Page in Book   Correct answer (written in the form of a statement using stem of question)

_____

_____

_____

_____

_____

_____

_____

_____

_____

_____

_____

_____

_____

_____

_____

_____

I got most of these wrong because…

Psych Movie Review

Reviewer _____

What chapter in the book is this movie most appropriate for? _____

The topic(s) it cover(s): _____

Identify some of the key characters in the movie that embody psych concepts in the chapter. Describe how their psychological issue(s) affect the storyline in the early part of the film.

_____

_____

_____

_____

What was the "low point" for the main character(s) in the movie? Did the psych issue cause that low point / crisis to occur?

_____

_____

By the end of the movie, it is probable that whatever crises or effects the psychological issue was causing was resolved in some way. Explain how this turn of events came about:

_____

_____

_____

Rate this movie from 0-3: _____

3: it was intellectually stimulating and entertaining
2: it had good points but was rather dull
1: it seemed misleading or irrelevant
0: it was not worth seeing- waste of time

One image or scene that stuck out was:

_____

_____

_____

Why did you rate it the way you did?

_____

_____

Would you recommend this movie to Friends or relatives outside of psych class?

_____

_____

_____

Psych Documentary Review

Reviewer _____

What chapter in the book is this documentary most appropriate for? _____

What topics does it cover? _____

According to the documentary, what are some old and new breakthroughs and discoveries in this particular field of psychological research? What implications does the new research hold?

OLD   **NEW**

_____

How does the material presented in this documentary piece affect your life or the lives of people around you? Do you see yourself making any material changes to your life as a result of what this documentary has been discussing?

_____

_____

Rate this documentary from 0-3: _____
3: it was intellectually stimulating and informative
2: it had good points but was rather dull
1: it seemed misleading or irrelevant
0: it was not worth seeing- waste of time

Why did you rate it the way you did?

_____

_____

One image or scene that stuck out was:

_____

_____

_____

Why do you think this particular scene was more memorable than the rest?

_____

_____

_____

Any final thoughts on this documentary?

Yale Lecture Review

Reviewer _____

Verify the right lecture to see with this chapter.
Go to http://antarcticaedu.com/opencourses.htm, and click on Bio Science.
Click on the first one under Psychology, the 'Yale' lectures, and make your selection.

Prof. Bloom is talking to college students who are somewhat familiar with the basic concepts in each chapter. His lectures are meant to illustrate the concepts. Review the vocab for the chapter you are working in first.

What topics does Prof. Bloom discuss in this lecture? Which concepts does he use to discuss those topics, and what examples does he use? You should note at least three topics, and at least ten concepts and examples for a full lecture. Use the vocabulary where appropriate.

TOPICS	CONCEPTS	EXAMPLES

How did Prof. Bloom's lecture change or influence the way you think about these topics?

Psychsim Tie-Ins

TOPIC	PSYCHSIM
Week 1: history, approaches	
Week 2: nature-nurture, subfields	Psychology's Timeline
Week 3: scientific attitude, surveys	Descriptive Statistics
Week 4: correlation, experiments	Correlation, What's Wrong with this Study
Week 5: neurons	Neural Messages
Week 6: brain	Brain and Behavior, Hemispheric Specialization, Dueling Brains
Week 7: behavior genetics	Mind Reading Monkeys
Week 8: sensation, eye	Colorful World
Week 9: perception, other senses	Visual Illusions, Auditory System
Week 10: sleep, dreams	EEG and Sleep Stages
Week 11: drugs	Your Mind on Drugs
Week 12: classical conditioning	Classical Conditioning, Maze Learning
Week 13: operant conditioning	Operant Conditioning, Helplessly Hoping, Monkey See/Monkey Do
Week 14: memory	Iconic Memory, Short Term Memory, Forgetting Trusting Your Memory, When Memory Fails
Week 15: cognition, language	My Head is Spinning
Week 16: motivation	Hunger and the Fat Rat, Catching Liars
Week 17: emotion, stress	Expressing Emotion, All Stressed Out
Week 18: childhood development	Conception to Birth, Cognitive Development
Week 19: adult development	Who Am I?, Signs of Ageing
Week 20: Freudian personality	
Week 21: other personality	
Week 22: intelligence testing	Get Smart
Week 23: nature of intelligence	
Week 24: anxiety disorders	Mystery Client
Week 25: mood and other disorders	Losing Touch with Reality
Week 26: psychotherapy	Computer Therapist
Week 27: biomedical therapy	Mystery Therapist
Week 28: social psych, conformity	Everybody's Doing It
Week 29: obedience, role adoption	Social Decision Making
Week 30: prejudice, altruism	Dating and Mating, Not My Type
Week 31: careers, at work, animals	

*You can access these lab tutorials by Googling: MyersAP1e (or if you want the added ones for the second edition then MyersAP2e). You can also access more by Googling: Psychinquiry.

Direct URL for Psychsim is: http://bcs.worthpublishers.com/myersap2e/default.asp
Direct URL for Psychinquiry is: http://ebooks.bfwpub.com/psychinquiry

Summer Assignment

AP PSYCHOLOGY SUMMER ASSIGNMENT

*** You'll need your own lined paper to do this assignment ***

GO TO ANTARCTICAEDU.COM/PSY.HTM AND CLICK ON THE GROOVIEST MOST FAR OUT WEBSITE (2ND ONE DOWN). Click "Want to Score a 5" and then on "Trippy Text"

This site was put together by AP Psych teachers and is a good source that will remain with us all year as we study our 14 chapters (one every two weeks).

1-7. Click Introduction and read through it. On a separate sheet of paper, discuss in complete short answer sentences the seven schools of psychology and how they would explain aggression in people (like Stewie from Family Guy). How would they diagnose or figure out what is wrong with him? What would be their object of investigation?

When done with 1-7, go back and click on Psychoanalytic School. This is Freud's way of doing psychology from the 1920s.

8-10. On your paper, discuss (8) the id, ego and superego, (9) what free association is, and (10) how Freud has been criticized. Click back and go to Behavioral School.

11-13. On your paper, discuss (11) what classical conditioning is, (12) what operant conditioning is, and (13) what observational learning is. Go back and hit Cognitive School.

14-16. On your paper, discuss (14) the perspective of the cognitive school, (15) Ellis' contributions (theories/discoveries) and (16) Beck's contributions. To back to Humanistic.

17-20. On your paper, discuss (17) what determinism is, (18) what freewill is, and (19) which one you agree with more: the Behaviorists that say our behaviors are determined by the environment around us, or the Humanists who say we have the freewill to dominate the environmental forces acting on us. Please give an example from your own life of how you or someone you know either was 'controlled' by their environment, or 'controlled' it. (20) Draw Maslow's Hierarchy of Needs and label it. Go back and hit Biological School.

20-22. From the perspective of Neuroscience: (20) what are three places our emotions/feelings come from? (21) Draw a neuron and label it. (22) Describe what each part you labeled does in one sentence. Go back and go to Cognition.

23-27. What (23) are the 4 kinds of cognition (mental activity) we will study? (24-27) Introduce (summarize) each of them- what are they? Go back and hit Abnormal.

28-34. Make a list (28) of anxiety disorders and look it up online (ex. Wikipedia page). Describe each disorder and name a famous person who have been diagnosed with that disorder. Do the same with (29) somatoform disorders, (30) dissociative disorders, (31) mood disorders, (32) personality disorders, (33) schizophrenia, and (34) the 'others'.

35. Go to psychmovies.com and look through the list of movies about psychology. Make a list of up to 5 that you have seen OR would like to see.

You're done! Have a great rest of the summer, and if you have any questions, send me an email at:

Best Bets Online

Kahoot.it can be a fun review game. Make a free account and the students can compete using their smartphones. Search for AP Psych jeopardy-style quizzes. Appsychology.com is a very good site with an informal, accessible style. Students can use it as a summary of the chapters in the text and for review.

Psychologytoday.com magazine has a whole lot of articles on most subjects, and a database of local psychologists for most metropolitan areas. Students can search for them by zip code, and see what fields they specialize in. Have students find things to read by hovering over 'topics' or using the search box.

On CharlieRose.com, a famed interviewer talks to people working in psychology (as well as most other fields) and you can search by topic. Ted.com/talks has psych related speakers.

Look for prison psychologist Theodore Dalrymple's articles on City Journal, New English Review and The Spectator magazine. Everything he writes is worth reading.

The Myers' Psychology for AP book site has tutorials that go with almost every chapter. This program is called Psychsim and comes with printable lab worksheets. it is best found by typing MyersAP1e into the search box, or for the new edition, MyersAP2e.

For more labs, try PsychInquiry as a search term, and a whole index will come up that you can select from. http://ebooks.bfwpub.com/psychinquiry/

On Youtube, search for Crash Course Psychology for reviews, as well as the many clips suggested above and others. You can download the video if your school blocks Youtube, and bring the clips in on an external hard drive.

As Myers is the most widely used textbook now, and has been for a generation, which textbooks were most popular two and three generations back? In the 1950s when behaviorism was at its height, it was Engle's *Psychology* (1955), and later, at the cusp of the neuroscience revolution, it was Ragland and Saxon's *Invitation to Psychology* (1985). Both of these books cost about 5 bucks on Amazon or Abebooks, and for perspective's sake are probably worth obtaining.

==

Thank You!

If this resource book has no use for you, it has no value. We strive to make materials you can actually *use*. No waste, no filler, only usable resources with minimal marginalia aligned with the course for convenience. This is how *Tamm's Textbook Tools* works:

Coursepak A, the *Assignments* series, one you already have, has daily assignments for Monday and Tuesday (or two other days of the week, however you work it). It has the vocab, people and chapter work covered.

Coursepak B, The *Bundle* series, soon available on *Amazon* and elsewhere, has material that can be used other days during the week. This time the focus is reading comp., online activities, multimedia, video clip response forms, short answers, primary sources and free response questions (FRQs).

Coursepak C, The *Crossover* series, is the part of the *Tamm's Textbook Tools* line that stretches across the disciplines. If you teach Social Studies and want to do get an integrated curriculum crossover going with the English department, or Math, Science, Liberal Arts, or other area of the school, you would look for the particular *Crossover* workbooks that fit best. All *Crossovers* weave in material from a variety of subjects in the way your subject relates to them.

Look for these and more in the *Tamm's Textbook Tools* series, a low-cost, timesaving way to find high quality, custom materials tailor made to textbooks in many different subjects. Contact the marketing department anytime with suggestions, corrections and any other correspondence at hudsonfla@gmail.com. Find *TTT* on Facebook as well. Please inform your colleagues of the existence of this series if you think one of our workbooks would benefit them. Thank you.

Made in the USA
Columbia, SC
22 September 2021